Pioneers of the Internet

Other Books in the History Makers Series:

America's Founders
Artists of the Renaissance
Astronauts
Cartoonists
Civil War Generals of the Confederacy
Civil War Generals of the Union
Cult Leaders
Dictators
Disease Detectives
Fighters Against American Slavery
Gangsters
Great Authors of Children's Literature
Great Composers
Great Conquerors
Great Male Comedians
Gunfighters
Home Run Kings
Influential First Ladies
The Kennedys
Leaders of Ancient Greece
Leaders of Black Civil Rights
Leaders of Women's Suffrage
Magicians and Illusionists
Male Olympic Champions
Native American Chiefs and Warriors
Pioneers of the American West
Presidential Assassins
Presidents and Scandals
Rock and Roll Legends
Rulers of Ancient Egypt
Rulers of Ancient Rome
Scientists of Ancient Greece
Serial Killers
Spies
Twentieth-Century American Writers
Women Inventors
Women Leaders of Nations
Women of the American Revolution
Women Olympic Champions
Women Pop Stars

Pioneers of the Internet

By Harry Henderson

Lucent Books
10911 Technology Place, San Diego, CA 92127

On Cover: Vinton Cerf (upper left), Marc Andreessen (upper right), Tim Berners-Lee (center), Jerry Yang (lower left), Jeff Bezos (lower right).

Library of Congress Cataloging-in-Publication Data

Henderson, Harry, 1951–
  Pioneers of the Internet / by Harry Henderson.
    p.   cm. — (History makers)
  Includes bibliographical references and index.
  Summary: Discusses the history of computers, the Internet and World Wide Web, navigating tools, and electronic commerce, with an emphasis on developers and entrepreneurs in the field.
  ISBN 1-56006-956-2
  1. Telecommunications engineers—Biography—Juvenile literature. 2. Internet—Biography—Juvenile literature. [1. Internet. 2. Businesspeople. 3. Computer industry.] I. Title. II. Series.
  TK5102.54 .H45 2002
  004.67'8—dc21

2001003774

CONTENTS

FOREWORD   6

INTRODUCTION
Inventors and Entrepreneurs   8

CHAPTER 1
Two Revolutions   12

CHAPTER 2
Vinton Cerf: Building the Internet   23

CHAPTER 3
Tim Berners-Lee: Weaving the World Wide Web   34

CHAPTER 4
Marc Andreessen: Netscape Changes the Landscape   46

CHAPTER 5
Jerry Yang: Gateway to the Web   57

CHAPTER 6
Jeff Bezos: The World's Biggest Bookstore   70

CHAPTER 7
Pierre Omidyar: Commerce Through Community   83

Notes   94
Glossary   99
For Further Reading   101
Works Consulted   103
Index   106
Picture Credits   111
About the Author   112

FOREWORD

The literary form most often referred to as "multiple biography" was perfected in the first century A.D. by Plutarch, a perceptive and talented moralist and historian who hailed from the small town of Chaeronea in central Greece. His most famous work, *Parallel Lives*, consists of a long series of biographies of noteworthy ancient Greek and Roman statesmen and military leaders. Frequently, Plutarch compares a famous Greek to a famous Roman, pointing out similarities in personality and achievements. These expertly constructed and very readable tracts provided later historians and others, including playwrights like Shakespeare, with priceless information about prominent ancient personages and also inspired new generations of writers to tackle the multiple biography genre.

The Lucent History Makers series proudly carries on the venerable tradition handed down from Plutarch. Each volume in the series consists of a set of five to eight biographies of important and influential historical figures who were linked together by a common factor. In *Rulers of Ancient Rome*, for example, all the figures were generals, consuls, or emperors of either the Roman Republic or Empire; while the subjects of *Fighters Against American Slavery*, though they lived in different places and times, all shared the same goal, namely the eradication of human servitude. Mindful that politicians and military leaders are not (and never have been) the only people who shape the course of history, the editors of the series have also included representatives from a wide range of endeavors, including scientists, artists, writers, philosophers, religious leaders, and sports figures.

Each book is intended to give a range of figures—some well known, others less known; some who made a great impact on history, others who made only a small impact. For instance, by making Columbus's initial voyage possible, Spain's Queen Isabella I, featured in *Women Leaders of Nations*, helped to open up the New World to exploration and exploitation by the European powers. Inarguably, therefore, she made a major contribution to a series of events that had momentous consequences for the entire world. By contrast, Catherine II, the eighteenth-century Russian queen, and Golda Meir, the modern Israeli prime minister, did not play roles of global impact; however, their policies and actions significantly influenced the historical development of both their own countries and their regional neighbors. Regardless of their relative importance in the greater historical scheme, all of the figures chronicled in the History Makers series made contributions to posterity; and their public achievements, as well as what is known about their private lives, are presented and evaluated in light of the most recent scholarship.

In addition, each volume in the series is documented and substantiated by a wide array of primary and secondary source quotations. The primary source quotes enliven the text by presenting eyewitness views of the times and culture in which each history maker lived; while the secondary source quotes, taken from the works of respected modern scholars, offer expert elaboration and/or critical commentary. Each quote is footnoted, demonstrating to the reader exactly where biographers find their information. The footnotes also provide the reader with the means of conducting additional research. Finally, to further guide and illuminate readers, each volume in the series features photographs, two bibliographies, and a comprehensive index.

The History Makers series provides both students engaged in research and more casual readers with informative, enlightening, and entertaining overviews of individuals from a variety of circumstances, professions, and backgrounds. No doubt all of them, whether loved or hated, benevolent or cruel, constructive or destructive, will remain endlessly fascinating to each new generation seeking to identify the forces that shaped their world.

Inventors and Entrepreneurs

Although the beginnings of the Internet date back to the late 1960s, most people learned of it only in the mid-1990s when a particular Internet application, the World Wide Web, became popular. In just a few years the Web grew from a tool for laboratory scientists to a global force used for education and commerce. The people who created this new technology have many ideas in common with the inventors who launched the first Communications Revolution back in the nineteenth century.

Inventions start with an idea about how to use the laws of nature to manipulate the physical world. In the 1840s Samuel Morse realized that the newly discovered properties of electromagnetism could be used to carry information along a wire. He proceeded to invent the telegraph. About thirty years later, Alexander Graham Bell discovered how to turn sound into patterns of electrical current, and he brought forth the telephone. Meanwhile, Thomas Edison sparked off one invention after another including the electric light, electric power systems, the phonograph, and motion pictures.

However, in the industrial world that arose with the harnessing of steam power and steel construction in the early nineteenth century, it was not enough to have a good idea or even to create a working invention. The inventor also had to persuade the government or private investors that the invention could be useful and thus profitable. In other words, the inventor had to become an entrepreneur, speaking not just the language of science and engineering but that of business as well.

But translating ideas into plans for a new business or industry can be as challenging a task as inventing new items. After all, the full implications of a new invention are seldom obvious from the beginning. For example, although government or military officials might see the value of linking telegraph lines from the nation's capital to other key cities, it took a further vision to see that Morse's new invention could also enable growing businesses to manage a network of offices and help railroads to safely guide dozens of trains.

Blazing New Trails

Very few people can visualize how a new invention might ultimately change daily life. Legend has it that when a small town mayor saw a demonstration of Bell's telephone, he exclaimed that it was surely a useful device, and that someday every town would have one. Indeed, even in the early 1950s, when J. Presper Eckert and John Mauchly began to market UNIVAC, the first commercially available digital computer, most business experts thought there might be a market for perhaps fifty of the huge machines, but surely no more.

What distinguishes the great inventors and entrepreneurs from the "might have beens" is that they can inspire people to believe in the possibilities of new technology and invest the money and effort to make them a reality. The Internet pioneers of the late twentieth century did just that. In doing so, they launched a revolution that is reshaping our social and economic landscape.

A technological revolution usually begins with some physical machinery, such as a steam engine or a computer. But what makes it a revolution is not only the technology, but also the new ways in which it can be applied. Thus Vinton Cerf and his colleagues created a system through which different models of computers on different networks could exchange messages. Once this Internet technology was in place, other pioneers could develop ways to organize and share information over the network. Tim Berners-Lee developed a program that organizes and manages a stream of data, formatting it so it can be retrieved and displayed by users connected to the Internet with desktop computers. He called it the World Wide Web. Soon many universities and research laboratories were using the Web to make information and resources available on-line.

Cerf and Berners-Lee were primarily inventors, although they displayed the skills of entrepreneurs in persuading colleagues to accept the technical standards they were proposing. But as the revolution began to shift from technology to applications, the role of the entrepreneur became more prominent. Thus programmer Marc Andreessen had to become a business entrepreneur. He had to convince investors that they could make money by giving away a Web browser and then selling the server software that would enable businesses to use the Web to advertise and sell their products and services.

Just as explorers often start out from base camps left by previous expeditions, the Internet pioneers have continually built upon each other's work. Once the Internet, the World Wide Web, and Web-browsing software were in place, entrepreneurs looked for ways to build successful businesses by using the network to deliver information, goods, and services. Each of these innovators had to create a business model—a plan for finding the right customers, marketing goods or services to them, and earning enough profits to keep the business running.

For example, Jerry Yang realized that the millions of new Web users would flock to a website that could organize the many topics of information into logical categories. He hoped that companies would be willing to pay to advertise on his Yahoo! website. Other entrepreneurs sought to sell goods rather than information. Jeff Bezos launched a Web-based bookstore where users could find, read about, and order books. The result was Amazon.com, now touted as "the world's largest bookstore."

Besides finding new ways to sell traditional products, Internet innovators have also found new ways to bring buyers and sellers together. Pierre Omidyar created the eBay auction website, making it possible for millions of people to buy and sell everything from collectible figurines to home entertainment equipment. He thus tapped in to a demand that had always existed but could not be served until the advent of eBay.

Who Are the Internet Pioneers?

The pioneers who shaped the Internet and on-line business have come from a variety of backgrounds, reflecting the global diversity of today's economy. For example, Pierre Omidyar is of Iranian descent, Jeff Bezos was raised by a Cuban American stepfather, and Jerry Yang was born in Taiwan. They also vary in their family's economic status and in their educational background. (Some have advanced degrees and others barely graduated from college.) But despite their diverse backgrounds, the Internet pioneers tend to have similar personal characteristics and life experiences.

While still in elementary or high school, they encountered computers and became fascinated with their potential. They tended to be interested in science and science fiction, preoccupied with the products of their imagination but often appearing to classmates to be in a world of their own. Yet even though Vint Cerf suffered from hearing problems and Jerry Yang arrived in America with little knowledge of the English language, they and the other Internet pioneers developed formidable communications and social skills. After all, whether one is trying to convince computer engineers around the world to adopt a single communications standard or attempting to sell investors on a business plan for selling books on the Web, the ability to speak persuasively and to persist despite rejections and setbacks is essential.

Each successful pioneer is an idea generator and can follow through with a plan and a vision that attracts the people who together make it possible.

With the Internet and related technologies changing so rapidly, it is impossible to predict what the next "big idea" will be or what kind of business might attract the interest of investors and the general public. But it is a pretty safe bet that the people who pioneer new Web applications will share many of the characteristics of this first generation of pioneers.

CHAPTER 1

Two Revolutions

Over the past century and a half, two revolutions have profoundly changed the way people interact with each other and with their world. The Communications Revolution linked the world with the telegraph, telephone, and radio. The Information Revolution standardized information processing and led to the programmable computer with its ability to store and manipulate vast quantities of data. About thirty years ago the two revolutions began to come together through the creation of computer networks. Eventually, this combination of telecommunications and data storage became today's Internet.

The Communications Revolution

The Communications Revolution began around the middle of the nineteenth century with the invention of the electromagnetic telegraph. Samuel Morse's telegraph used a simple code of dots and dashes to represent the letters of the alphabet. Today's computers use a similar code to store characters, except they replace the dots and dashes with ones and zeros. Thus in both the telegraph and today's computer networks, information is transmitted in binary pulses carried electrically.

Though early telegraph signals traveled at the speed of light, they were too weak to go more than a few miles. Messages to more distant destinations had to be relayed from one operator to another. However, inventors such as Thomas Edison designed devices that could record incoming messages, making it easier to relay them forward. This "store and forward" method of passing messages from point to point to a final destination is much like the way e-mail and other data is sent over the Internet today.

Only ten years after Morse sent his famous first message "What hath God wrought?" thirty thousand miles of telegraph wire had been strung across the United States. The telegraph system grew so fast because people discovered that certain kinds of information—such as stock or commodity prices—were more valuable if they could be received sooner. The telegraph was also an ideal companion to the railroad, which was revolutionizing the movement of people and goods. Using the telegraph, railroads could keep track of their many trains and route them efficiently.

When the telegraph was still in its infancy, the pioneering American writer Nathaniel Hawthorne wrote his novel *The House of the Seven Gables*. One of its characters, an elderly man named Clifford, describes the significance of the new communications medium. He exclaims that

> By means of electricity, the world of matter has become a great nerve, vibrating thousands of miles in a breathless point of time. . . . Rather, the round globe is a vast head, a brain, instinct with intelligence! Or, shall we say, it is itself a thought, nothing but thought, and no longer the substance which we deemed it![1]

By the 1880s the telegraph had changed the way businesses operated. Undersea cables linked the financial markets of New York and London, and money could be wired easily from one bank to another. News dispatches arrived at newspaper offices almost as quickly as events happened, stock markets reacted, and updated prices flashed over the wires to stock tickers.

The telegraph, however, did not go in to people's homes. People could not use it to communicate directly; they had to go to a telegraph company and pay to transmit the message, which then had to be delivered from the destination office to the recipient. However, as the nineteenth century drew to a close, a new invention, the telephone, was beginning to democratize communication. Although expensive and unreliable at first, by the mid–twentieth century the telephone had spread to every office and home, aided by automatic switching systems that had replaced the old operators and their plug boards.

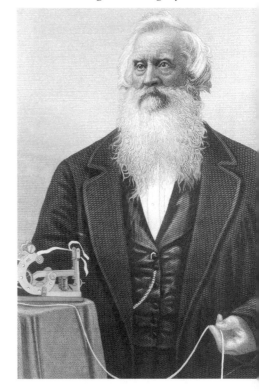

Using a simple code of dots and dashes, Samuel Morse demonstrated his invention of the electromagnetic telegraph.

The Information Revolution

By the 1940s the telephone had given most people in America access to high-speed communications. But as the population grew and the economy became larger and more complex, both government and business struggled to keep up with a growing torrent of information: orders, bills, checks, receipts, reports, insurance policies, licenses, medical records, and much more. The ability to communicate quickly and to transport goods by railroad or truck helped business grow. But the need to store, retrieve and manage all the information represented by all those pieces of paper also grew greater every year.

In the earlier part of the nineteenth century British mathematician and inventor Charles Babbage conceived of a way to apply the machinery of the Industrial Revolution to the processing of information. He described plans for an "Analytical Engine," a machine that could use numerous intricate gears to store numbers, perform complicated calculations with them, and even print out the results. The machine would receive instructions in the form of codes on punched cards. Although building such a machine proved beyond Babbage's capabilities, its design foresaw all the essential features of today's computers.

Babbage's ideas were largely forgotten, but by 1890 American inventor Herman Hollerith had devised machines that could read and tabulate data from census cards, helping the government count 100 million Americans in far less time than using the old manual methods. By the 1940s offices used various kinds of electromechanical tabulating machines and calculators, many made by a company called International Business Machines (IBM). This equipment helped people manage data, but it was neither automatic nor fast enough to keep up with the growing need for information.

Recreation of part of a Charles Babbage calculating "engine."

Birth of the Modern Computer

World War II made the need for rapid information processing even more urgent. Logistics, the management and distribution of military supplies, generated huge quantities of records. Artillery guns were useless without data tables specifying how to aim them under varying conditions. Breaking German and Japanese codes offered the United States and its allies an advantage over the enemy but the machine-made codes seemed unbreakable.

J. Presper Eckert operates the Universal Automatic Computer (UNIVAC), a calculating machine used for the census.

In 1939 the U.S. government gave a contract to Harvard researchers led by Howard Aiken. They built a huge room-sized calculator called Mark I. Although it was impressive, the machine relied on mechanical relays like those used in the telephone switching system. It was faster than human mathematicians, but not really fast enough.

To increase the speed of calculation, J. Presper Eckert and John Mauchly used vacuum tubes to generate the pulses that make up the ones and zeros of binary numbers. Because vacuum tubes use electronics rather than moving parts to control data flow, their machine, called ENIAC, could calculate thousands of times faster than the Mark I. By the early 1950s a commercial version, UNIVAC, was in use in government offices, large corporations, and a few universities.

The Revolutions Come Together

Electronic computers offered the promise of finally catching up to the flood of information being generated by modern industrial society. But once information was generated by a computer, it could be communicated only by shipping stacks of punched cards or printouts.

Somehow the tools of the Communications Revolution had to be made available to those of the Information Revolution.

Unfortunately, getting computers to talk to one another was far from simple. Thanks to the telephone system, a universal, standard network for carrying electromagnetic signals was already in place. It was not even that difficult to build a device that could convert the ones and zeros in computer memory to pulses that could travel over the phone lines—today such a device is called a modem, and most PCs (personal computers) usually include one as standard equipment.

But the computers of the 1950s were not designed to communicate with other computers. Rather, they were set up only to give instructions to peripheral devices such as printers. For example, it was as though someone had grown up knowing the meaning of English words and how to form sentences, but without ever having spoken to another person. Further, one had to imagine an English-speaking person who met another person who spoke only Chinese. The problem was that computers from different makers usually had different internal "languages." They stored data differently, using different patterns of bits to store numbers or characters. Finding a common language for computer communication seemed to be an almost hopeless task.

Just as the needs of World War II had spurred the development of the electronic computer, the needs of the cold war between the United States and the Soviet bloc led to the funding of another U.S. government computer project. The government used giant computers to monitor chains of radars and plan defense against enemy bomber or missile attacks. In 1957 the Soviets shocked America by launching *Sputnik*, the first satellite to orbit Earth. It seemed only a matter of time before the Soviets would have nuclear missiles capable of destroying American defense computers.

Building Computer Networks

In 1958, the year after *Sputnik* launched, the U.S. Defense Department established the Advanced Research Projects Agency (ARPA). Its general mission was to invest in the development of new technology that might give the United States an advantage in future wars. One of its research areas was the design of a computer network that could potentially survive even a nuclear attack.

Fortunately, the researchers and engineers challenged to design such a network could draw upon new developments both in electronics and in computer design. By the 1960s the introduction of the transistor was making it possible to build computers that were smaller (refrigerator-sized rather than room-sized), faster, and more reliable. Using these "minicomputers," university researchers began designing operating systems that allowed several users to share the same computer. Both hardware and software were becoming more adaptable to the use of computers as communications devices. In 1962 J. C. R. Licklider wrote a series of memos that described the social possibilities for people logging on to computers to share ideas and information in what he called a "Galactic Network."[2] The challenge was finding an efficient way to organize such a network.

The previous year Leonard Kleinrock, an ARPA researcher, published the paper "Information Flow in Large Communication Nets." He sketched out the architecture for a computer network. He explained that "The nets under consideration consist of nodes, connected to each other by links. The nodes receive, sort, store and transmit messages that leave via the links."[3] In other words, any computer could send a message to any other computer in the network. The message might pass through several intermediary computers, much as the old telegraphers relayed messages from one station to the next. However, there was still the problem of transmitting a message from the Pentagon to a radar or missile control computer if an enemy attack had destroyed several of the intermediary links.

At RAND Corporation, a research think tank, electronic engineer Paul Baran suggested an answer to making networks that could withstand even severe damage. Ordinary communications networks such as the telephone system use a routing method called circuit switching. Each communication (such as a phone call) is switched into a particular circuit or line. If the line fails, communication is lost. In his paper "On Distributed Communication Networks," Baran suggested "that messages be broken into units of equal size and that the network route these message units along a functioning path to their destination where they would be reassembled into coherent wholes."[4] In this system, called packet switching, the computers would keep track of all the possible routes between two computers. If the direct route between, for example, the UCLA computer center in Los Angeles and the Stanford Research Institute in the San Francisco Bay area was not available, messages could still be routed by way of another computer, perhaps one in Utah or Nevada.

Because it might enable computer networks to survive in wartime, ARPA adopted the idea of packet switching, and in 1967 researcher Larry Roberts wrote the plans for a network that came to be known as ARPAnet. Creating a general-purpose network would require hardware that computers could use to process the data packets and send them over the phone lines. Bolt, Beranek and Newman (BBN), an electronics company based in Cambridge, Massachusetts, was given the contract to build a device called an Interface Message Processor, or IMP, which was actually a minicomputer in its own right. The finished devices were made of heavy-gauge steel to military specifications (this was, after all, an ARPA project), and weighed nine hundred pounds each. The refrigerator-sized IMPs even had eyebolts that could be used to hoist them using a crane or helicopter.

In the course of four months in late 1969 Kleinrock and other ARPA researchers connected four computers, each with its own IMP. These first four network "nodes" (computer locations) were built at the University of California at Los Angeles (UCLA), the Stanford Research Institute (SRI), the University of California at Santa Barbara (UCSB), and the University of Utah. Although the four machines were all different models, the researchers wrote custom software to translate the messages to and from a common format as they flowed between the computers and IMPs.

Kleinrock recalls the day they sent the first network message, a request from the UCLA computer to log in to the SRI machine:

Leonard Kleinrock's research in packet switching provided the technological foundation of the Internet.

What was the first message? "What hath God wrought?" Or, "Great step for mankind!" No. All we tried to do was log on from our host to their host. Remember—we're engineers. So I had one of my guys, Charlie Kline, set this up and we also had a voice line in parallel [following the same route as] over the data line. He had a pair of headphones and a speaker and so did the other guy at the other end. You want to type in LOG and the rest would span out: "LOG IN." And so we typed in L. And we said, "Did you get the L?" And he said, "I got the L." Typed the O. "You get the O?" "I got the O." "You get the G?" Crash! The system failed on the G. A couple hours later we successfully logged in, did some minimal things, and logged off. That was the first message on the Internet. "Log in, crash." [5]

From Network to Internet

Even when they got it to work, the ARPA researchers knew that their hard-wired, handcrafted network was only a temporary solution. Many separate networks were being created by computer manufacturers. But if IBM mainframes could talk only to other IBM mainframes, or DEC (Digital Equipment Corporation) minicomputers could talk only to others of their kind, data communications would be as unsatisfactory as the early days of the telephone, when offices often needed a separate phone for each phone company.

In 1974 Vint Cerf and Robert Kahn announced the Transmission Control Protocol (TCP) and Internet Protocol (IP). A *protocol* is a set of rules that specify how an activity is to be carried out. In computing, a protocol describes how data will be organized and processed. A data communications protocol also instructs what a computer should do when it receives a specific instruction from another computer. As long as all computers follow the rules, they could communicate with one another.

TCP/IP works in a manner similar to letters being sent through the mail. If a letter or package is properly addressed, the post office can route it to its final destination even if it has to be carried on a truck, a plane, and then another truck. Similarly, each packet of data on the Internet includes a header that specifies its sender and destination. A computer called a router can determine the most efficient way to send data to its destination, even if it must pass through several different computers.

By the end of the 1970s many universities were starting to connect to the new Internet. A system called USENET (or Netnews) enabled users to post messages (called articles) that were automatically forwarded from one computer to the next. The messages were organized by servers into topical categories called newsgroups, and users could "subscribe" to a newsgroup and read the latest news and ideas. A standard e-mail system also made it possible for individuals to send messages to one another.

Internet usage grew steadily through the 1980s, though because the network was pretty much limited to universities and the computer industry, most Americans were not aware of it until an accidentally released "worm" program clogged up the system by automatically copying itself from one computer to another, causing widespread outages in 1988.

At the end of the 1980s the Internet was undoubtedly already useful, but it was also hard to use. Accessing information meant running a variety of different programs and typing in text commands. The Internet had great potential but only if it could become as universal and accessible as the telephone.

The World Wide Web

In 1989 Tim Berners-Lee, a researcher at the CERN, the European physics center, started to analyze the problem of organizing the information that his fellow researchers were generating and storing on hundreds of incompatible computers. Although the Internet had the potential to put all these computers in touch with each other, one program was needed that would connect to all the different sources of information on the Internet and display it in convenient screens of text. Berners-Lee adopted the idea of *hypertext* first suggested by the visionary computer scientist Vannevar Bush in 1945. Using hypertext, information on one page could be linked to another page—even a page stored on an entirely different computer. By following links, the reader could find footnotes, supplementary information, or related writings. A special language called HTML (Hypertext Markup Language) would be used to specify how the pages would be linked and formatted. This new system was called the World Wide Web. But if the Web were to become truly "World Wide," it would have to be made accessible to millions of computer users.

By the 1990s the personal computer had become an increasingly common item not only in offices but in schools and homes as well. Using a modem, a PC user could dial up information services such as CompuServe or America Online. These services were attractive and relatively easy to use, but they were not connected to the Internet. The World Wide Web offered a way to bring the greater resources of the Internet to ordinary consumers, but the most common existing Web-browser programs worked only with text. However, programmer-entrepreneur Marc Andreessen developed a graphics-based browser called Mosaic for the National Center for Supercomputing Applications (NCSA). He then started his own company and created an improved version called Netscape, which could be downloaded to Windows and Macintosh computers for free. Netscape not only showed graphics, but it also used "plug-in" utility programs to play sounds and show animation.

A New Marketplace

Thanks to the popularity of Netscape (and a rival program from Microsoft called Internet Explorer), the Internet and World Wide Web were no longer restricted to universities, research labs, and computer companies. Many Internet Service Providers (ISPs) sprang up to offer Internet connections to home users. America Online and other services expanded their offerings to include Internet access and Web browsing. More and more schools began to connect their classrooms to the net as well.

By the mid-1990s entrepreneurs were rushing onto the Web to offer goods and services to businesses and individual consumers. Among the early innovators were Jeff Bezos, whose Amazon.com offered more different titles than could fit in any physical bookstore, and Pierre Omidyar, whose eBay auction service let anyone buy or sell almost anything on-line. A company called Webvan even offered on-line ordering of groceries and other items for convenient home delivery. People can now shop for everything from airline tickets to computer equipment to home mortgages.

One of the most important goods sold on the Web is information itself. Many newspapers and TV networks offer current news and other features for free, hoping to encourage people to subscribe to the full publication. "Web portals" offer a user-friendly way to find Web sites in hundreds of categories. (The oldest and largest portal is Yahoo!, started by Jerry Yang and David Filo.)

Investors poured millions of dollars into new "dot-com" businesses (named for the .com in their Web addresses). For a while, it seemed that any idea, no matter how outrageous, would be funded. However, late in 2000 investors became more nervous about whether any of these new companies would really be profitable, and prices of dot-com and other tech stocks dropped significantly. The stock market downturn particularly hurt corporations devoted to a purely Internet-based business model. According to the e-commerce

Dr. Vannevar Bush (far left) designed analog computers. His idea of hypertext information links helped inspire the creation of the World Wide Web.

research company Webmergers, 222 major Internet companies closed in 2000, and by mid-2001 another 269 had folded. In the second quarter of 2001 twelve companies canceled their plans to offer their first public stock, and many other companies announced job cuts. And in July 2001 Webvan's trucks stopped rolling as the company filed for bankruptcy.

Nevertheless, worldwide Internet usage is still growing as developing nations join in, and the total value of goods and services sold on the Web in the United States in 2001 is expected to be $34 billion, rising to $104 billion in 2005. Companies will come and go, but the twin revolutions in communications and information processing have merged for good, forming the foundation for twenty-first–century commerce and education.

Along the lines that once clattered with dots and dashes, a torrent of text, images and sounds can now be tapped in every office, school, and home. Who knows what the next generation of inventors and entrepreneurs, growing up with mouse in hand and "www" on their lips will someday accomplish.

CHAPTER 2

Vinton Cerf: Building the Internet

Like most great technological breakthroughs, the Internet is the product of many different creative minds working on a common problem. However, when historians look for the person whose vision and guiding influence shaped the Internet through the first decade of its existence and beyond, they usually give Vinton "Vint" Cerf the title of "father of the Internet." They do so because Cerf (pronounced Surf) not only developed the technology for a new form of computer communications, but he also used his personal communications skills and leadership to persuade people to accept and help develop his ideas. He combined his insight into technology with the stamina needed to work with his ideas until they could be made into realities.

For his vision and guiding influence in shaping the Internet, many historians consider Vinton Cerf the "father of the Internet."

A Slow, Deep Learner

For someone who would play so important a role in developing communications technology, the young Vint Cerf seemed not to communicate all that well. Born on June 23, 1943, in New Haven, Connecticut, he was the first of three sons of Muriel and Vinton Thruston Cerf. According to his mother, the boy developed "slowly and unevenly," so much so that his parents thought that he might have a mental defect. But as his mother notes, "One day as he was playing in the sandbox, I suddenly realized that what I was looking at was not mental retardation but a long attention span and quiet, self-contained maturity."[6]

Later, doctors discovered that Vint had suffered a birth defect that had damaged his hearing in both ears. Despite his handicap, Vint became a top student in grade school. His fifth-grade teacher gave him a seventh-grade algebra test to take home for the summer, and he solved every problem. He enjoyed chemistry and created "volcanoes" of plaster of Paris and potassium permanganate that sputtered and fumed. Like many other boys at the dawn of the Space Age, he also became interested in model rocketry. These interests suggested that although he was quiet and a little shy, Vint was not afraid to tackle new, exciting, and perhaps risky technology.

A Passion for Programming

Vint became involved with another new technology that he found to be as exciting as rockets but not as glamorous. As a fifteen-year-old high school student he first glimpsed a computer, a vacuum-tube monstrosity that filled three whole rooms. Although it intrigued him, he did not have an opportunity to take a closer look. Two years later, however, he and his friend Steve Crocker, even though still in high school, received permission from a sympathetic UCLA official to use the university's Bendix G-15 computer. "The bug had bit, and I was infected by computers,"[7] he would later recall. The reason for his "infection" with computers was a sense of power that he felt when he programmed the machines: "There was something amazingly enticing about programming. You created your own universe and you were the master of it. The computer would do anything you programmed it to do. It was this unbelievable sandbox in which every grain of sand was under your control."[8]

Cerf wanted to spend as much time with the machine as possible, but because the two boys were still in school, they were free only on weekends. However, one Saturday they arrived to find the building locked. "I couldn't see any choice but to give up and go home," Crocker remembered. "Next thing I knew, Vint was on my shoulders."[9] From that vantage point Vint was able to climb in through a window and unlock the door from inside, taping the latch so they could go freely in and out of the building.

Cerf's preoccupation with computers was not the only thing that made him different from most other high school students. He later described his appearance in high school, where he wore a sports jacket and carried a big briefcase, as "maybe a nerd's way of being different."[10] Although he was somewhat of an outsider in school, he did feel a deeper connection to the world as a whole. As a youngster he made the realization that "the whole universe was hooked together."[11] This sense of interconnection proved useful when it came time to link computers and their users together.

Beginning to Communicate

After high school, Cerf went to Stanford University and graduated in 1965 with a degree in math. He then worked at IBM as an engineer on new computers that allowed many users to share the same machine. But he decided he needed a more thorough background in the new field of computer science, so he entered the graduate program at UCLA, where Steve Crocker was finishing his degree. Crocker's adviser, Jerry Estrin, had the ARPA contract for the "Snuper Computer"—a program that would allow one computer to log into another computer and monitor its activity. (This ability to run programs from one computer on another is a key part of networking.) Estrin hired Cerf as a research student, and Cerf wrote his doctoral thesis on remote computer monitoring. Gradually he was learning the technologies and skills he would need for building computer networks.

While working with computer communications, Cerf also learned to deal with his personal communications problems. He wore a hearing aid in each ear. One day, when visiting his hearing aid dealer, he met a young woman named Sigrid Thorstenberg, an illustrator and interior designer who was also hearing impaired. Unknown to Cerf, the dealer had arranged their appointments so they would meet, thinking they might make a nice pair. A year later they were married.

Meanwhile, the pace of Cerf's computer work was speeding up. In 1968 the project to create ARPAnet, the Defense Department–sponsored computer network, was officially under way. Although ARPA was a government agency with the objective of developing new technology for the military, it gave its researchers considerable leeway to explore a variety of ideas, even those that might seem to have little practical application. There was much brainstorming about the possible uses of the emerging computer network. Steve Crocker recalls that he, Vint Cerf, and the other engineers "found ourselves imagining all kinds of possibilities—interactive graphics, cooperating processes, automatic database query, electronic mail—but no one knew where to begin." [12]

Testing the Network

It was time to move from brainstorming and theory to building a practical networking system. Leonard Kleinrock, a pioneer in computer networking, set up a Network Measurement Center for the purpose of designing and testing ideas for computer networks. Cerf became one of the senior members of a team of forty software engineers that comprised the growing project. He describes the trial-and-error approach that they took:

> I had the fun of working on the network measurement center for Arpanet. My job was to figure out how the system was performing and to overload it in order to find out how it would respond—whether it broke or fought back. We managed to destroy the network on several occasions by deliberately launching too much traffic. That was part of the research—to understand how the technology would function. [13]

Leonard Kleinrock set up the Network Measurement Center for the purpose of designing and testing ideas for computer networks.

Based on the results of their tests, Cerf and his colleagues began to connect computers to form a network. By 1970 a tiny network was in operation, linking together four computers in different cities and using specially written software that allowed a user on one machine to log in to another. This was a far cry from a system that would allow any computer to seamlessly communicate with another, however. They still needed a universal, consistent language—a protocol—that any computer could use to communicate with any other computer on the network.

Cerf and his colleague, MIT researcher Larry Roberts, set out to design such a system, using the packet-switching idea that Leonard Kleinrock had introduced back in

Special "black boxes" called routers now enable mass networking between room-sized Internet Service Providers.

1961. Kleinrock suggested that computer data could be broken up into tiny "chunks," relayed across a network and then reassembled into its original form.

However, to make this idea work, they would have to devise a system of headers and addresses to identify packets and their destinations. They would then have to write a program that could read the addresses and route the packets efficiently through the network to their destination. Special computer devices called "black boxes" (later called routers) connected to each network computer would store information about the different possible routes from that computer to the other computers (nodes) to which it would be directly connected. The program would have to quickly determine which node to send an outgoing packet to, considering such factors as line speed, congestion, or circuit failures. If a packet does not reach its next destination, it would have to be resent. If it still did not get through, an alternate route would be tried. Writing software that could cope with changing conditions and still maintain acceptable speed was quite a challenge.

By 1972 ARPAnet was in high gear with dozens of universities and other research centers trying to bring their computers onto the network. Cerf and his colleagues feverishly prepared for the International Conference on Computer Communication, scheduled to take place in October at the Hilton hotel in Washington, D.C. Again, Cerf showed the ability to deal not only with theory and engineering, but also with practical details and the coordination of a team effort. To make their demonstration work, the network team installed special phone lines and set up dozens of computer terminals. Because they did not have enough equipment of their own, they used whatever they could beg, borrow, or buy. "It was just an amazing experience," Cerf recalls. "Hacking away and hollering and screaming and saying 'No, no . . . you got this one wrong.' Getting all the details right." [14]

Arranging all the parts in a single computer to work reliably was difficult enough. But as soon as someone started to connect computers, many other factors came into play, including the condition of phone lines hundreds or even thousands of miles away—lines designed to carry voice messages, not precise computer data. If two people are speaking over a long distance and a bit of static drowns out one of their voices, the other person can simply ask "What did you say?" Programming computers to keep their conversation going after a disruption of their carefully timed signals was much harder.

However, all their frenetic work paid off. The demonstration was successful and served to create much interest in ARPAnet while raising Cerf's own professional stature. He was soon made chair of the International Network Working Group, and he also became a professor of electrical engineering at Stanford. He made the move from engineering to teaching network fundamentals to the upcoming generation of computer engineers. He also coordinated the planning and establishment of standards for what would soon become a worldwide network.

Setting the Standards

While working at Stanford, Cerf and his colleague Robert Kahn, an expert on network operating systems, officially announced in 1973 the new network protocol that they had demonstrated, called TCP/IP. But they faced the challenge of coordinating the practical implementation of TCP/IP and of convincing other people to adopt it for their own networks. By this time many different computer makers and research centers had invested considerable effort in networking, with the networks based on different operating systems (such as IBM, DEC, and Unix). Devising a way for these different networks to communicate with each other required not only that each network implement TCP/IP, but also that special hardware called a gateway be set up to translate messages from one computer data format to another. Together with Kleinrock and Kahn, Cerf became one of the key "evangelists" promoting the use of TCP/IP not only for mainframes and minicomputers, but also for the desktop PCs that came on the market in the 1980s. In each case he tried to show computer manufacturers how their products would benefit from sharing data with other kinds of computers.

Throughout this effort, Cerf's ability to organize meetings, coordinate efforts, and persuade people to cooperate showed how the awkward high school programmer had become much more socially adept. In a paper titled "Confessions of a Hearing-Impaired Engineer," Cerf humorously noted that he had applied engineering principles to the problem of following a conversation when he could not hear all of it:

> A typical strategy here is to dominate the conversation, not by doing all the talking, but by asking a lot of questions. In this way the deaf listener will at least know what question the speaker is addressing, even if he cannot hear all of the response. [However] in a group conversation this can backfire embarrassingly if the question you ask is one which has just been asked by someone else. A variation (equally embarrassing) is to enthusiastically suggest something just suggested. [15]

Cerf was also willing to use humor to get people's attention. At one meeting where engineers were debating the merits of using IP for their computers, he performed a sort of striptease. As he recalls, "[I] removed my coat, waistcoat, tie, and finally my dress shirt. Underneath was a T-shirt that read 'IP on Everything.'" [16]

By 1977 the use of IP had spread widely indeed. Demonstrating the global scope of the network and its ability to use many different kinds of communication, Cerf sent a signal four hundred miles from the Bay area to southern California, relaying it by means of a mobile communications van with a packet radio link, then onto ARPAnet throughout America and Europe, then up to a satellite link and down to a receiver in Los Angeles for an eighty-eight-thousand-mile round trip using three separate networks.

Throughout the 1970s and into the 1980s Cerf continued to work tirelessly. He promoted ARPAnet and helped the technology keep up with the ever-increasing load on the system as new institutions joined it, and it eventually became known as the Internet. Cerf claims that "The Internet really was my responsibility in a very absolute sense from '73 to '82." [17]

Shaping the Internet

Meanwhile, Cerf had gone to work for MCI in 1982. He helped this big new telephone company develop connections to the rapidly growing on-line world, including establishing an e-mail service. Although he did valuable and satisfying work as an industry consultant, Cerf was soon drawn back into guiding the future of the Internet. In 1986 he joined his colleague Robert Kahn at the Corporation for Research Initiatives, where they developed new standards and plans to expand the Internet.

In 1992 Cerf helped found the Internet Society and became its first president. The organization ensured that the people who had contributed the most to the development of the network would continue to play an important role in coping with the challenges that the growth of the Web would bring. Like many of the Internet pioneers, Cerf became concerned with difficult social issues arising from the extension of the Web into schools and homes. He worried that poorly drafted legislation that attempted to protect people from net abuses such as pornography or fraud could damage the free flow of information that is the network's essence. He opposed many proposals for government regulation of the network:

Vint Cerf (far left), Robert Kahn (far right), and their colleagues discuss the social implications of the Internet.

I'm most concerned about heavyhanded intervention to attempt to regulate the Net. Although the Supreme Court struck down the Communications Decency Act, some members of Congress are trying to revive similar legislation. . . . I've often traveled to Capitol Hill to brief Congress on the industry, and I'm struck at just how misinformed some members are concerning the Internet. Thankfully this is changing, although not as fast as I would like. [18]

However, Cerf does not oppose all government involvement with the Internet. He points out that it was government funds that paid for the development of the net in the first place. He has also argued that Carnivore, an FBI program designed to sift through e-mail to find evidence of criminal activity, was safe to use because it was designed to only gather information specified in a court order.

Cerf's career has spanned the Communications and Information Revolutions. For the future, he sees them being more closely intertwined:

Think of the Internet and the Plain Old Telephone System, or POTS, as two tapestries hanging side by side. The Internet is dynamic and flourishing, while the phone system is venerable, ubiquitous, and reliable. Now imagine if we take these tapestries apart and reweave them together one strand at a time so the two are indistinguishable from one another. That's the future we're heading toward. [19]

Cerf believes that by 2010 even ordinary phone calls will travel over the packet-switching system of the Internet. But perhaps by then the Internet will be woven so deeply into all the devices and activities of daily life that people will no longer think consciously about the technology, just as people today seldom think about the technology that sends their phone calls through cables and bounces them off satellites.

Cerf renewed his lifelong interest in science fiction in 1998 when he began to help the Jet Propulsion Lab (JPL) in Pasadena, California, plan to extend the Internet beyond the earth into the far reaches of the solar system. In the proposed "Interplanetary Internet," satellites, space stations, space probes, and eventually, astronauts voyaging to Mars and beyond, would have Internet addresses to guide communications and the flow of data from other worlds.

"Elder Statesman" of the Internet

As the Internet's relatively young "elder statesman," Vint Cerf continues to educate the public and his fellow professionals about the problems and possibilities of a still-emerging technology. Cerf's boss during

President Bill Clinton awards Vint Cerf and Robert Kahn the National Medal of Technology.

his MCI years sums up the influence of the man who had guided the development of one of the twentieth century's greatest achievements:

> Vint is many things and is probably as close to a Renaissance man as there is in the 21st century. He is part scientist, engineer, philosopher, businessperson but perhaps, most of all, a great teacher. Not just in the sense of imparting information, which he does very well, but in making you think and looking at not just networks but life in a whole new perspective. [20]

Vint Cerf has received many of the highest awards in computer science, but perhaps his most treasured award came in 1998 when he received the Alexander Graham Bell award for his contribution to improving the lives of the deaf and hearing impaired. When he received the award, Cerf noted that "As an individual who is hearing-impaired, I'm extremely proud of the level-playing-field result the text-based Internet has had on communications among hard-of-hearing and hearing communities alike." [21]

In his long and varied career, Vint Cerf has demonstrated the key characteristics that would mark later Internet pioneers. He had the imagination to see how the power of computers could be multiplied by enabling them (and their users) to communicate with one another. He had the engineer's attention to details that was essential for keeping complex projects on track. He has proven to be not only a builder of communications devices, but he is also a communicator himself. He has made difficult ideas clear to thousands of students and colleagues. In creating and supervising the "plumbing" that makes the Internet work, he has shown that he is a leader who inspires people to work together to turn ideas into reality.

CHAPTER 3

Tim Berners-Lee: Weaving the World Wide Web

Back in the 1960s, a young British boy named Tim Berners-Lee noticed a rather curious old encyclopedia on his parents' shelves. Entitled *Enquire Within upon Everything*, it offered knowledge and advice on what seemed to be every subject in the world. As he read and learned at home and school, Tim became intrigued by the connections between bits of knowledge. An imaginative yet methodical person, he would eventually make it his life's work to find ways to use computers to link facts and ideas together. The result of his persistence is the World Wide Web. Today, the Web is revolutionizing commerce, education, and daily life. Thanks to Tim Berners-Lee's pioneering ideas, people can now point, click, and "enquire within upon everything."

Growing Up with Computers

Tim Berners-Lee's interest in technology was not really that surprising, given his family background. He was born on June 8, 1955, in London. In the early 1950s his parents were both mathematicians with the programming team for Manchester University's Mark I, one of the world's first general-purpose digital computers. "Computer talk" was thus part of Tim's daily world, and it inspired him to build pretend computers out of cardboard boxes. He cut slots in them and ran his parents' discarded punched paper tape through them to mimic the operation of the computers at his parents' workplace.

In addition to computers, mathematics was another common household topic. The family often played number games around the breakfast table. At an age where most schoolchildren were still learning their times tables, young Tim had already become acquainted with advanced mathematical concepts such as the "imaginary numbers" used to describe negative square roots. Tim's knowledge of mathematics soon surpassed that of his classmates.

By the time he began high school at the Emanuel School in London in the early 1970s, Tim's interests had expanded to include electronics. At that time microprocessors (computer chips) were just starting to become available, and the popular electronics magazines were beginning to speculate about the possibility of building something called a "micro-computer"—a computer that could sit on a desktop instead of filling up most of a room like the ones his parents had used at Manchester University. Although ready-built microcomputers were still a few years away, Berners-Lee studied circuit plans and wired a microprocessor together with logic circuits and an old television set. In doing so, Tim demonstrated his ability to visualize the parts of a system that did not yet exist and, step by step, turn it into something real. This set the pattern he would use for tackling the information problems that would eventually lead to the World Wide Web.

Although Berners-Lee enjoyed working with computer hardware, he became even more interested in arranging the data stored inside the machine. He once saw that his father was hard at work, and asked him what he was doing. His father said that he was writing a speech about the possibility of making computers that could link ideas together in the way the human brain did. Tim, intrigued by such possibilities, eagerly discussed them with his father. Later, Tim would pursue these

Tim Berners-Lee's pioneering ideas for the World Wide Web revolutionized commerce, education, and daily life.

ideas about linkage in creating a "web" of information on the computer. First, however, he needed to gain the detailed knowledge he would need to truly master computers.

Berners-Lee went to Queen's College at Oxford University, where he received his physics degree with honors in 1976. His work in physics brought him into contact with physicists and other scientists who were having trouble keeping up with the torrent of data coming from their experiments. The problem of managing scientific data soon brought him back to the world of computers.

After graduating, Berners-Lee worked on various projects for computer companies. For one project, he developed software for a new kind of computer printer. In getting the printer to work, he became familiar with ways to represent fonts (styles of type) in documents. He would use this knowledge later to help him design the software that displays Web pages in a browser. He also gained experience in developing operating systems, the complex programs that manage the flow of data in computers.

Science's Tower of Babel

The road that would take Berners-Lee to the World Wide Web began in 1980 when he was hired as an intern at CERN, the giant particle physics laboratory in Geneva, Switzerland. CERN was facing a growing "information overload." With as many as ten thousand scientists from around the world constantly coming, going, or moving from one project to another, the laboratory was finding it very difficult to keep track of who was connected to what. Without some way to organize the information about all the scientists' activities, it was hard to schedule the use of the lab's busy computer facilities or to coordinate their efforts.

CERN also had another communications problem. Often, scientists from different countries spoke different languages; their computers had different "languages" as well. Many scientists brought their own software to help them analyze data, and the different programs were written to run on different computers and operating systems. If one scientist created a graph or chart with one program, another scientist who used different software might not be able to use the data. The scientists' efforts were often frustrated by the difficulty in sharing data and ideas. The need to find a common language for sharing data pushed Berners-Lee toward creating a new way of organizing information.

CERN tried to use databases (collections of files containing data records) to keep track of each person's assignment and the computers and software he or she was using. The traditional way of working with

CERN, the atomic research installation in Geneva, Switzerland where Berners-Lee first conceived the idea of the World Wide Web.

data was to have a program search through the file looking for a matching record. Thus, searching the user file could find the record for Scientist "A." Searching through the file of computers or programs could find a particular machine or piece of software. But it was not easy to answer a question such as "what computers does Scientist A use?" or "Who are the scientists who are using Computer B?"

Following the Links

Berners-Lee's interest in "enquiring within" and the linking of knowledge suggested a possible solution to the problem of finding information in databases. As he had learned from his father, the human brain does not retrieve data the way most computers do. If someone asks a person whether he or she has any pets, the person's brain does not search through a long list of household objects, looking to see if any of them are domestic animals. Instead, the brain forms a sort of web of connections between nerve cells. Through a mechanism not yet fully understood, the brain can follow a maze of links to retrieve images, words, sounds, or ideas. Thus a mental image of a dog chasing a squirrel might come to mind, or perhaps the sound a cat makes when demanding food.

"Suppose," Berners-Lee wondered, "all the information stored on computers everywhere were linked? Suppose I could program my computer to create a space in which anything could be linked with anything?"[22] In other words, could a computer store and retrieve information not as a database did, but as a brain did? He demonstrated a way to do this by writing a small program to answer questions about data. He later recalled that it would keep "track of all the random associations one comes across in real life and brains are supposed to be so good at remembering but sometimes mine wouldn't."[23] He named his program Enquire after the childhood encyclopedia that had inspired him.

In Enquire, Berners-Lee arranged it so that each piece of information (such as the description of a person, a software package, a project, or a computer system) has links to other relevant information. For example, if a particular scientist works with a particular computer, his or her record would include a link (or address) from which one could retrieve the record for that computer. Similarly, if a user were looking at the record for a computer, he or she could use its links to review the records of the people using that machine.

Berners-Lee's creation of the Enquire program showed that he looked at a problem (such as information retrieval) in a way very different from the conventional approach. He methodically created a system that applied his ideas to actual data.

From Data to Information

Philosophers sometimes make a distinction between *data* and *information*. Data is raw facts or numbers. To become information, data must have a context or relationship to other facts. Computers often simply collect data and leave it up to people to dig out the relevant information. Berners-Lee believed that Enquire created a system for automatically turning data into information:

> The program was such that I could enter a new piece of knowledge only if I linked it to an existing one. For every link, I had to describe what the relationship was. For example, if a page about Joe was linked to a page about a program, I had to state whether Joe made the program, used it, or whatever. Once told that Joe used a program, Enquire would also know, when displaying information about the program, that it was used by Joe. The links worked both ways.[24]

Enquire impressed some of Berners-Lee's colleagues, but as an intern, his main job was to work with the systems that recorded data from experiments. He did not have the opportunity to create a complete system to share data between scientists. But, as with the idea of

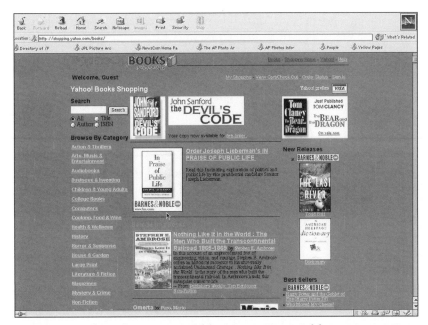

Web pages such as the one pictured here are transmitted between computers using Berners-Lee's HTTP protocol and formatted using his HTML language.

building his own computer, once he had a vision, Berners-Lee perservered. After his internship at CERN ended in December 1980, Berners-Lee worked for a software company on a variety of projects including graphics and instrument control systems. However, he continued to explore the idea of linked information.

The Hypertext Solution

In 1984 Berners-Lee received the opportunity to return to CERN as part of its permanent staff with responsibility for developing new information systems. The laboratory's information-coordination problems had grown worse, but now he would be able to tackle them head on. Although the idea of linked bits of information was promising, using Enquire would mean taking all the existing databases (such as address and phone directories) and converting them to Enquire's format of nodes and links. Because this would be a time-consuming task, Berners-Lee instead decided that any system he developed would have to take documents as they were and link them, rather than changing them all to the same format.

Berners-Lee began to look more closely at an intriguing way to organize documents—a system called "hypertext." The idea in hypertext is that any word or phrase in one document could be used as a link to another part of the document—or an etirely different document. For example, in the sentence "**Volcanoes** are clear evidence that the world

39

beneath the earth is constantly changing," the reader could link from the word **volcanoes** to another document giving more information about that subject.

Berners-Lee decided that hypertext offered the best way to add links to documents and make them available over the network. He needed a system that was simple enough that users could create and link their own documents, and he needed several versions of the program that could run on all the major kinds of computer systems.

From his earlier work with printers and type formatting, he was familiar with the idea of a "markup language" that specified how the text in a document should look. He wrote a simplified version of such a language, which he called Hypertext Markup Language, or HTML. This language used "tags" written in ordinary text to mark parts or features in the document.

Linking to the Internet

By the late 1980s Berners-Lee had developed a way to link text documents. But he also needed a method for the links to travel from one computer to another. Fortunately, he had already developed a program called remote procedure call (RPC) that let computers link to programs on other computers. However, he needed to figure out what kinds of computer networks his hypertext system would run on. If he wanted to serve only CERN's needs, he could write his programs so that they used CERN's network. However, an increasing number of computers at college campuses and research labs in the United States and elsewhere had adopted the Internet. Indeed, the Internet was starting to become the worldwide network that linked all other networks. Berners-Lee decided to make sure his RPC program and the rules for accessing documents (called HTTP, or Hypertext Transfer Protocol) would work with the Internet. Again, he refused to take the easy but limited approach. He remained true to his vision of a system that would be open to the widest possible participation.

The final key to putting hypertext on a network was creating a unique address for every document. For this purpose Berners-Lee devised the URI (Universal Resource Identifier), which later became known as the URL (Uniform Resource Locator). These are the now familiar Web page addresses such as http://www.microsoft.com/ms.html.

The Web Proposal

Some people excel at technical tasks; others are good at inspiring people. Then there are those who can do both, and Berners-Lee was one of them. For his ideas to gain acceptance, Berners-Lee had to convince CERN (and eventually, computer users around the world), that it was worthwhile to create, link, and use hypertext documents.

In March 1989 Berners-Lee issued his official proposal to the CERN community, emphasizing the ease of use and utility of the new system. With hypertext and links, he told users that they could "create a common base for communication while allowing each system to maintain its individuality. . . . All you have to do is make up an address for each document or screen in your system and the rest is easy." [25] Because the system was intended to extend its links until they spread around the world, he called it the World Wide Web.

Launching the Web

At first there was little reaction at CERN to Berners-Lee's proposal. Perhaps this was because the idea of a networked hypertext system was too unfamiliar to scientists accustomed to using traditional databases. People were a bit slow to grasp the possibilities.

Berners-Lee decided that the only way to get any real response to his ideas was to implement them. With some help from assistants, he wrote the two key programs needed to make the Web a reality: a server and a browser. The server would accept requests and addresses and send the requested pages of information over the network. The browser allowed the user to view documents, click on hyperlinks, and fetch the documents from the server. A small number of colleagues tried browsing the infant Web.

Huge servers (background) and browsers (on computer) were the final tools that made the Web a reality.

At the end of 1991 Berners-Lee traveled to San Antonio, Texas, where he demonstrated the Web at the trade show "Hypertext '91." Again, he was called upon to be resourceful. At the time, Internet access was not widespread: It was available mainly through universities. Undaunted, he strung a phone line from the exhibit hall to the college campus so he could log on and connect to the main website at CERN.

By 1992 it had become clear that Berners-Lee's enthusiasm for the Web was becoming contagious. Because he had written a system that could be used by any program that followed the rules, other people were able to write Web browsers for other kinds of computers. As word spread, more people were starting to put their own websites online.

Making Choices

During the 1990s entrepreneurs such as Marc Andreessen started businesses creating Web software and setting up on-line services. As inventor of the Web, Berners-Lee could have become a highly paid consultant or perhaps even started an on-line company of his own.

Instead, Berners-Lee again demonstrated his persistence of his vision of a universal Web. He believes that "My primary mission was to make sure the Web I had created continued to evolve. There were still many things that could have gone wrong. It could have faded away, been replaced by a different system, have fragmented, or changed its nature so that it ceased to exist as a universal medium . . . for sharing information." [26]

The growing commercial interest fueled the development of the Web and helped make it accessible. But commercialization also threatened the ideals behind the Web. One fear was that one or a few companies could gain control and create a Web that was available only to its own customers. And if companies started writing incompatible browsers or different versions of HTML, the Web might lose the very purpose for which it had been invented: the universal, unfettered exchange of information. Berners-Lee was determined to ensure that the purpose would not be lost.

Steward of the Web

Because he believed that industry and developers had to maintain a common standard that would keep the Web available to all, Berners-Lee founded the World Wide Web Consortium, or W3C, in July 1994. This group brought together people who shared many of his ideals and visions. Their goal was to make sure the Web stayed true to these visions as it grew.

Berners-Lee speaks at a W3C conference, explaining the necessity to keep a common standard for Web development.

By the mid-1990s the Web began to appear in schools and homes. Millions of dollars of business were being carried out through Web pages. The Web was starting to have a considerable impact on the way people lived, shopped, and traveled, for example. Although he was interested in the technical development of the Web, Berners-Lee was equally concerned about the social impact of its use. He felt that everyone working with the Web had to take responsibility for dealing with the new issues that were arising. At the first World Wide Web conference at CERN, Berners-Lee ended his technical talk by pointing out that "like scientists, people in the Web development community [have] to be ethically and morally aware of what they [are] doing." [27]

Berners-Lee educated government leaders about the realities of the Internet, and he worked with his fellow Web developers to respond to social concerns such as the growing amount of pornography being posted on the Web.

Berners-Lee tried to explain why regulators could not treat the Internet in the same way they had treated other media such as television:

It [censorship] is very difficult to achieve because the Internet allows information to flow in many different ways. You are only a small hole in this vast system. In a way, controlling or regulating information is bad for the relationship between a government and the people and, in the long term, for the stability of the country. [28]

Berners-Lee also believed that Internet users themselves could effectively address the problem of inappropriate Internet material. Although technology made the spread of undesirable material easy, it also made possible tools for users to control the content they received. He noted that schools and parents could use filtering software to block children's access to inappropriate content without reducing the diversity of expression on the Web as a whole.

Berners-Lee and the W3C also dealt with the important issue of protecting the privacy of Web users. Often, websites recorded information about what users were doing on-line without first seeking their permission. As a result, users could be flooded with junk e-mail or "spam." As with the censorship issue, Berners-Lee prefers improving the technology to imposing regulations. The W3C proposed setting up a standard by which websites disclose how they collect user information and what they intend to do with it. Users could then make an informed choice about whether to use a given website. As with censorship, Berners-Lee suggested that the best way to deal with the problems caused by the new information technology is to give its users more information so they can make better choices.

To control the use of personal information on the Web, Berners-Lee and the W3C developed the Platform for Privacy Preferences Project (P3P).

Whatever the particular issue, Berners-Lee has approached it with a central idea in mind. Deciding how the Web is to be used is as important as how the technology is to develop further. He insists that "The Web is more a social creation than a technical one. I designed it for a social effect—to help people work together—and not as a technical toy." [29]

Shaping the Future

The Web is now widely available and easy to use. But Berners-Lee has always pushed his vision one step further. He sees a future Web that will make it easier for ordinary users to create and edit their own Web pages. He believes that the true promise of the Web will be realized only when people collaborate and share ideas as easily as they pick up a phone.

Today it is possible to learn much from the Web by browsing or using a search engine. But Berners-Lee is still pursuing his father's dream of a brainlike computer with the ability to meaningfully link pieces of information. He continues to develop his ideas for a semantic Web where information is encoded so that software can roam the Web automatically, not merely looking for matching words or phrases, but following threads of meaning to bring back an answer to an inquiry about anything.

In creating the World Wide Web and helping to make it safer, easier to use, and more useful, Tim Berners-Lee has shown how imagination, resourcefulness, and persistence can turn a vision into a world-changing reality. For his achievements, in 1999 Tim Berners-Lee was named by *Time* magazine as one of the one hundred greatest minds of the twentieth century. The impact of his work will continue well into the twenty-first century.

CHAPTER 4

Marc Andreessen: Netscape Changes the Landscape

When Tim Berners-Lee developed the World Wide Web software, the versatile system for linking text across the Internet quickly became a useful tool for researchers in universities and laboratories. In the early 1990s the bulk of Internet users were still academics, students, scientists, and engineers. But in just a few years the Internet and the Web became household words familiar to millions of families. "Web surfing" became a popular activity, and the message "You've got mail" became the equivalent of an on-line answering machine.

For this to happen, however, the Web software would have to be transformed from a text-only display driven by keyboard commands to the graphical "point and click" screens familiar to millions of Windows and Macintosh users. Twenty-two-year-old student Marc Andreessen had the programming skill to do this. But he would also need to be an entrepreneur, someone who could create a business based on the new Web technology and attract investors and partners to make it grow. By combining both technical and business skills, he created the first "dot-com" or on-line company, doing business on the Internet.

Programming Prodigy

Marc Andreessen was born in 1971 in the small town of New Lisbon, Wisconsin. His father was a seed salesperson and his mother worked at Lands' End, a mail-order clothing company. When he was only about nine years old, Marc learned the BASIC computer language from a book he found in the library. He promptly wrote a program on the school computer to help him with his math homework. However, he didn't have a disk to save the program on so he lost all his work when the janitor turned the power off at the end of the day.

This misfortune did not discourage him from working with computers. Indeed, by seventh grade his parents purchased for him a computer so he could program whenever he wanted to. Marc continued his interest in computing in high school, where he wrote another program to help match his lonely friends with appropriate dates.

After high school, Marc enrolled at the University of Illinois to study computer science. He impressed his classmates as being more than a narrowly focused "techie," however. As one classmate recalled, "Marc just seemed to have a broader sense than the rest of us. Say we were talking about God or something. He would talk about it in a more complete way, with more than one view. And we'd sit back on our heels and say, 'Wow, oh yeah.'" [30] Later, a writer would be equally impressed by Andreessen's mental dexterity: "A conversation with Andreessen jumps across a whole range of ungeekish subjects, including classical music, history, philosophy, the media, and business strategy. It's as if he has a hypertext brain." [31] Andreessen's ability to think deeply, link ideas together, and present them in an attention-grabbing way served him well when it came time to create a new business.

Improving the Web

While working in the university's computer lab, Andreessen first encountered the Internet and Berners-Lee's World Wide Web. He realized there was a lot of interesting information on the Internet, but it was hard to use the software that retrieved it. As he recalled later, "The early days of the Internet were exciting, there were lots of things to be done, but it was originally elitist and only accessible to academics and researchers." [32] But the young programmer believed that could change. "Internet software was 10 years behind the hardware. I realized we could pull the software forward a few years." [33] If they could upgrade the software, then the Web would be accessible to millions of people, not just a select few.

In 1993, while still an undergraduate, Andreessen made $6 per hour as an intern at the National Center for Supercomputing Applications (NCSA). During his internship, he met programmer Eric Bina who shared his interest in improving the software that lets users read

By combining technical and business skills, Marc Andreessen created Netscape, the first major Internet-based company.

and browse Web pages. Bina's ability to deal with detailed technical tasks meshed well with Andreessen's ability to see the big picture of how program features would be experienced by users. Together with other volunteers, Andreessen and Bina wrote a browser called Mosaic.

The new Web-browsing program was colorful (it displayed graphics), easy to install, and easy to use. Because NCSA was a government agency and not a private company, it made Mosaic freely available to users and licensed it inexpensively to companies that wanted to sell it commercially. After only a year, 1 million copies of Mosaic had been downloaded by users from the Internet or distributed on floppy disks.

Forging a Partnership

Meanwhile, the young computer scientist wondered whether the popular Mosaic software could be used to establish a successful business. Later he recalled that "At the NCSA, the deputy director suggested that we should start a company, but we didn't know how. We had no clue. How do you start something like that? How do you raise the money?"[34] To find out how, Andreessen went to the heart of the computer industry.

In 1993 Andreessen finished the studies for his degree and then moved to Silicon Valley, the area just south of San Francisco where many of the world's most important computer companies have their headquarters. Silicon Valley was the most logical place to obtain capital for his new company. At first, he was unable to raise funds. But in early 1994, Andreessen received an e-mail that read: "You may not know me, but I'm the founder of Silicon Graphics. I've resigned and intend to form my own company. Would you be interested in getting together to talk?"[35]

That offer was rather surprising. It came from Jim Clark, who was more than twice Andreessen's age. Clark was a millionaire who had already made his fortune as a computer entrepreneur. He had turned Silicon Graphics into an extremely successful company that specialized in building high-powered desktop computers for creating the sophisticated 3D graphics used in movies such as *Jurassic Park*. Clark quit as CEO when his colleagues rejected his suggestion that the company start making lower-cost workstations for Internet users. Andreessen, on the other hand, was a talented programmer who created a remarkable program but had no previous business experience.

Andreessen and Clark met at Clark's home and then aboard his yacht. Despite their difference in age and experience, the two men found they had similar ideas. They soon agreed to form a company together. As writer Alison Sprout observes: "For Clark, the partnership was a chance to start over; for Andreessen, 23, it was a once-in-a-lifetime opportunity to form a company with a Silicon Valley legend."[36]

Jim Clark (left) sits with colleague Ed McCracken of Silicon Graphics. Clark left Silicon Graphics to form Netscape Communications with Marc Andreessen.

Clark invested $4 million of his own money to start operations. They moved to nearby Mountain View, California, and set up their company, which at first they called Mosaic Communications Corporation. However, the University of Illinois sued them, claiming that they owned the Mosaic name and had licensed the Mosaic software to another company called Spyglass. Andreessen and Clark renamed their company Netscape Communications.

Launching Netscape

However, the company name was the least of their worries. To make a Web browser that would take over the market, Andreessen would have to compete against his own program, the freely distributed Mosaic. But Andreessen was confident that his programming ideas would enable him to make a browser that would be faster, more reliable, and more graphics intensive. (Their desire to surpass Mosaic was reflected in the code name they gave their product while it was being developed: "Mozilla.")

Andreessen recruited many of his former NCSA colleagues for the new company. While working the eighteen-hour days that had become standard among young programmers, they finished the new program in only a few months. Their new browser was called Mosaic NetScape (later renamed Netscape Navigator). Not only was their new program faster and better looking than Mosaic, but it also anticipated the coming growth of Web-based business by including a feature that allowed users to send encrypted credit card information safely to websites. (This encryption prevented hackers from stealing credit card information by intercepting transactions.) Navigator was an instant hit, and soon it comprised more than 70 percent of the browser market. *Time* magazine named it one of the ten best products of 1994.

By 1995 *Time* and other publications were paying a great deal of attention to the World Wide Web. While experts began to debate whether the Web would transform business, the public became fascinated with the young entrepreneurs who were starting new Internet-based companies. As one of the first successful Internet entrepreneurs, Andreessen symbolized this new breed of innovator. Still only twenty-four years old, he looked more like a young rock star than a traditional businessperson. He often rejected business attire in favor of jeans and bare feet.

An instant hit, Netscape dominated 70 percent of the browser market.

In summer 1995 Netscape first offered stock to the public. The stock had originally been priced at $28 a share, but public interest was so high that it opened at $71 a share. By the end of the trading day the price had settled down to $58 a share and the total value of the company was $2.3 billion. This exceeded the value of established industrial companies such as Bethlehem Steel. Andreessen's personal portion of the stock was worth $55 million. On paper at least, he was now a very wealthy young man.

Netscape hired experienced executive Jim Barksdale to become its CEO, while Andreessen took the title of senior vice president of technology. Andreessen was described by Barksdale as the company's "principal technology visionary." [37] Both contributed to the company's public image: Barksdale assured investors that the company would be stable and prudent in its management, and Andreessen's continuing presence suggested that it would remain on the cutting edge of technology.

However, as Andreessen tried to shape the future direction of the company, he found that Netscape had a problem that would become rather familiar in later years as the Internet market boomed. The company was not actually making much money. After all, they gave away their main product, the browser, virtually for free. (Theoretically, everyone except students or educators was supposed to pay $39 or $49 for the browser, but it could be downloaded for free and "tried" indefinitely.) As one observer noted, Netscape's business plan was

> essentially the reversal of the venerable marketing strategy of giving away safety razors to sell blades. Netscape is basically giving away the consumer version of its program—the blade— in the hope of profitably selling and servicing the razors. The razors in this case include versions of the Navigator for companies that are operating sites on the World Wide Web. [38]

If Netscape were to succeed and meet the investors' expectations, it would have to sell a lot of software to companies that wanted to take advantage of the special features of Netscape on their websites. Netscape charged from $1,500 to $50,000 per site, depending on how many special features the customer wanted.

At first the company seemed to be on the way to success. Largely because of the way Netscape brought the Web to the attention of millions of consumers, many companies were now eager to offer their products and services through the Web. They included news services such as Knight-Ridder, publishers such as Hearst, and financial institutions such as Bank of America. Not only did these companies pay Netscape to set up their websites, but many also bought ownership shares in Netscape itself. After three years the company was taking in about $150 million a quarter (three months) and employed three thousand people. With Netscape, Andreessen had shown that it was possible to create an Internet company that could rival the biggest traditional companies.

The Biggest Challenge

But there was a shadow on the horizon. In *Star Wars* the intrepid heroes gulp when they first see the Death Star looming ahead of their tiny ship. For Marc Andreessen, as for much of the young generation of programmers, the Death Star was the software giant Microsoft. The multibillion dollar company dominated the desktop market by selling Windows, the operating system used on more than 90 percent of personal computers.

Microsoft chairman Bill Gates was surprised by the growing popularity of the World Wide Web. As Andreessen added more features to Netscape, some people thought it might become an operating system of its own, providing services such as e-mail and even running programs from the Web using a new programming language called Java. If so, Netscape, which could run on Macintosh computers and Unix machines as well as Windows PCs, might give software developers and users an alternative to Microsoft's operating system and office software.

Gates vowed that Microsoft, too, would become an Internet company and revise all its programs to work with the Web. Microsoft also began to develop its own Web browser, Internet Explorer. At first most software reviewers considered Explorer to be inferior to Netscape, but Microsoft steadily improved the program. And because Microsoft included or "bundled" Explorer with Windows, an operating system that PC makers already had to buy for each new machine, computer companies generally did not see a reason to pay extra for a copy of Netscape. Further, Microsoft offered free Web-serving software as an alternative to much of the software that Netscape was trying to sell to its clients.

However, Andreessen continued to show his resourcefulness and willingness to meet challenges. In a bold attempt to rescue Navigator, Andreessen decided to make the software "open source," meaning that unlike ordinary commercial software, the program language codes used to run Navigator were made available for anyone who wanted to improve the program or adapt it to other purposes. Open source has been quite successful in some areas, including development of Linux, a version of the Unix operating system created by Finnish programmer Linus Torvalds. Andresseen hoped that a corps of enthusiasts would keep Netscape in the forefront by adding features more quickly than the relatively cumbersome Microsoft could do with its Explorer browser.

But open source and other innovative ideas could not stop the decline of Netscape. Gradually, Microsoft usurped Netscape's lead and gained the dominant share in the browser market. Netscape and other companies accused Microsoft of unfairly using its monopoly on operating systems to lock competitors out of the market and urged the federal government to take legal action. In 2000 a federal court declared that Microsoft had violated antitrust (monopoly) law and Microsoft appealed the decision.

While the fate of the legal case remains unclear, the practical result was that Netscape was struck a devastating blow in the marketplace. By 1999 the company was running up debt and cutting back employees. However, its website, Netcenter, continued to attract many Web surfers seeking news and interesting links. America Online (AOL), the nation's largest online information service, saw an opportunity to combine Netscape's website (as well as its software for business websites) with its own products. That same year AOL bought Netscape for almost $10 billion and Marc Andreessen became AOL's chief technology officer.

Microsoft chairman Bill Gates became Netscape's leading competitor after creating Internet Explorer.

Starting Over

Andreessen did not stay long at AOL, however. Having made and carried out bold business plans at Netscape, he was now just part of a team whose goals were set by others. In September 1999 he resigned from AOL and a month later, he started a new company—LoudCloud. As he explained to an interviewer, starting a new company has its advantages and disadvantages:

> In a startup [a new company] you get to do whatever you want. You get a clean sheet of paper and can design whatever you want—make the world in your own image. But, saying that, startups are overromanticized. . . . I always find it to be a roller coaster of euphoria and depression, sort of in equal measures. At Netscape, I'd go home a lot of nights just completely depressed. Like, you know, "Oh, my God, we're going to go right out of business. There's not going to be any market for what we're doing. It's going to flop." Startups are a lot more emotionally tough and demanding than people believe—and therefore not quite as much fun as people think they are.[39]

Starting anew, Andreessen created LoudCloud, an Internet long-term consulting firm for large corporations.

Andreessen would have to balance his expansive imagination with a tight focus on practical business realities. In 2000 the great Internet "gold rush" ended. It was no longer enough to have a new idea: Investors wanted to be confident that an entrepreneur had a specific plan to make money. With LoudCloud, Andreessen decided to focus on what had been one of Netscape's strongest areas—the development of software and consulting services for corporations setting up business websites. Andreessen noted that Web software had become much more complex in recent years:

> Two years ago, with say, Amazon.com, it was getting more complex; they added shopping carts, one-click buying, and searching. Now you have all these features plus auctions, E-stores, and merchant circles [groups of cooperating merchants that are linked to one another]. And because it's the Web, you can roll out new features overnight, so the complexity of the software just ramps up at an exponential pace. [40]

Thanks to his success during the early years of Netscape, Andreessen had an outstanding reputation as an entrepreneur. The services LoudCloud offered were well suited to a booming Internet economy in which companies competed fiercely to establish sites where consumers could buy books, music, electronics, and other products.

Andreessen points out that LoudCloud has a different business approach from Netscape and other software companies. He notes that, "The financial model of a software company is you have to move on to your next customer, because you have to go get next month's revenue." [41] Unlike traditional software companies, LoudCloud focused on signing up large customers and developing long-term, profitable relations with them. By September 2000 the company had signed contracts with thirty companies to manage their websites. Each company paid somewhere between $50,000 and $500,000 a month for the service.

LoudCloud needed to raise a lot of money to pay for its equipment and programmers. In March 2001, Andreessen went on a grueling road trip, holding seventy meetings with potential investors in the Americas and in Europe. He hoped to build up interest in LoudCloud in preparation for its first stock offering. But by this time, the "dot-com" world was in turmoil, with even large, successful companies such as Yahoo! and Amazon struggling to be profitable. With a falling stock market, investors were much more reluctant to buy stock in new companies, even companies led by successful entrepreneurs like Marc

Andreessen. Andreessen was able to raise some money, but the stock sold for much less than anticipated.

Like the future of e-commerce itself, the fate of LoudCloud is uncertain. However, Marc Andreessen has shown throughout his career that he can combine an inventor's insight into the possibilities of technology with an entrepreneur's intense drive to succeed.

CHAPTER 5

Jerry Yang: Gateway to the Web

Tim Berners-Lee's World Wide Web provided the tools to link together information on computers all over the world. Marc Andreessen's Netscape browser brought the Web into many homes and schools. But as thousands of websites began to appear, it became clear that if the Web were going to be truly useful, people needed ways to find information.

Jerry Yang developed Yahoo!, the first service to organize the Web to make it easier to find information on any subject.

Web surfing, or following interesting links to see where they lead, could result in valuable finds, such as a historical archive or a site that compared prices and features for computer systems. But if a user needed something specific—say, a list of organizations devoted to women's health—it was hard to know where to begin.

By 1994 search engines such as Lycos appeared. Search engines work by sending little "bots," or robotlike programs to explore and trace out all the links on the Web. As the bot arrives at a website, it records significant words that it finds, as well as keywords included by the designer of the site. All the keywords and site addresses are compiled into a huge index. When users type in a word or phrase such as "women's health" the search engine scans its index and finds the sites that match those words. Search engines can return hundreds or thousands of results, leaving the user to explore them in a hit-or-miss fashion.

Chinese American student Jerry Yang helped millions of Web users. Aided by his partner David Filo, Yang created a well-organized list of categories under which the most useful and interesting sites on the Web were organized. If the Web was the world's library, Yang provided its card catalog. His site, Yahoo! (the exclamation point is part of the name), became the most popular gateway to the Web.

For Yahoo! to succeed, Yang had to create thousands of links to Web pages. But equally important, he had to forge personal links with the Web's many information providers. He created partnerships where both he and they could profit from the growing stream of Web users. In turning his ideas about information linking into a thriving business, Jerry Yang became a legendary figure for the young Web community.

A Quick Learner

On November 6, 1968, a boy named Chi-Yuan Yang was born in Taiwan. Chi-Yuan's father died when the boy was only two years old. His mother, Lily, taught English and drama. She noticed that her son was unusual. "Ever since he started to speak, he was very annoying, always asking 'What is this?' 'Why?'"[42] While many young children are inquisitive, this boy was exceptionally bright. He started to learn to read Chinese characters at three. This incessant curiosity was useful when it came time to surf the Web.

When Yang was ten, Lily brought him and his brother to the United States. Looking back, Yang recalls that the decision to move the family to another culture was risky and difficult. "It wasn't an easy decision for my mom . . . the ability to teach English wasn't exactly a skill that was in short supply in the U.S. So even though she had the language skills to get along here, she didn't have the slightest idea what she would do. She was really brave."[43]

The two boys were given Americanized names, Jerry and Ken. The family settled in San Jose, California where Lily worked as a maid. Jerry spoke very little English when he arrived in America. (The only word he knew at the time was "shoe.") But Jerry recalls that he soon mastered the school curriculum: "We got made fun of a lot at first. I didn't even know who the faces were on the paper money. But when we had a math quiz in school I'd always blow everyone else away. And by our third year, my brother and I had gone from remedial English to advanced-placement English."[44]

After graduation from high school, Yang went to Stanford University and majored in engineering. He enjoyed the rigorous work involved in engineering, but he also found time to participate in other

Jerry Yang (left) and David Filo (right) demonstrate Yahoo!'s capabilities for Secretary of State, Madeleine Albright, in 1999.

activities. He joined a fraternity as well as student government committees. None of these activities slowed him down academically, however. By the age of twenty-one he earned not only his bachelor's, but also his master's in electrical engineering. However, he decided that he was not yet ready to leave school and go to work. As he notes, "I had the degree of a Master's, but I didn't have the experience or the maturity. I was twenty-one, barely. Actually, not even. So I looked for ways to stay in school." [45]

Yang decided to do graduate research, perhaps leading toward a doctorate. He joined a research program that found ways to use computers to help design electronic circuits. There he met another graduate student, David Filo, and the two soon became good friends. However, the adviser who was supposed to supervise the two students had gone abroad on a research sabbatical, and they found it hard to stay focused. As a result, Yang remembers, "I was quasi [sort of]-retired at 23, playing a lot of golf." [46]

Besides playing golf, Yang and Filo spent a lot of time surfing the Web. By then Netscape was available, which made navigating the Web easy. But they soon found that while the Web had many fascinating pages, it was difficult to tell someone else about a good find. If someone found a site that had baseball statistics, for example, it might have an address of http://sports.espn.go.com/mlb/statistics. If the person mistypes a letter or two, he or she receives the dreaded "not found" message from their Web browser.

A Little List

In early 1994 Yang decided to end his frustration of keeping track of Web pages. He created a Web page called "Jerry's Guide to the World Wide Web," listing his favorite websites. (Later David Filo added his own favorites, and the list became "Dave and Jerry's Guide to the World Wide Web.") As Yang added more sites, he divided the list into topical categories to make it easier for the growing number of visitors to their website.

The growing legions of new Web users were hungry for any help in their search for information. By the summer of 1994 the list had 1 million "hits" (or accesses) a day. Yang and Filo's e-mail box filled with messages from people asking about sites or offering their own "finds." The phone, too, rang all day and all night long—because the Web was indeed becoming "worldwide," stretching across many time zones.

Yang had originally created the list for his own benefit and as a free service for whoever wanted to use it. But he had started something new just as entrepreneurs were starting to build Web-based businesses. As Yang later recalled:

> In 1994 we heard about Netscape Communications being funded and how they were releasing Navigator as a commercial product. It was amazing how many Internet startup ideas were being generated within a very close community of friends at school. And for a while, we were sitting there literally writing business plans for Internet-based businesses while on the side working on [what would become] Yahoo, thinking, That's never going to be a business. So we did shopping malls. We did booksellers. We actually designed a system where you could inventory and order books, similar to Amazon.com today.
>
> But at the time, we didn't realize the thing that we'd been working on for fun was going to be the one that succeeded. But finally we realized that if we stopped, then all those people using Yahoo would go away and they wouldn't have anything. We felt we were offering a service that people really wanted. And that's what got us thinking about it as a business.[47]

Yang and Filo were further spurred to set out on their own when the Stanford administration complained that processing so many requests for their Web guide was putting too much of a strain on Stanford's server. Even though Yang and Filo were only three months away from completing their doctorate degrees, their Web work swallowed up nearly all of their time. Yang noted that:

> [We] ended up working about 20 hours a day on Yahoo and sleeping at the lab anyway, and it was hard to keep up. So we decided we had to do something—either shut it down or find a corporate sponsor to give us some servers and some bandwidth and some people, not so much to start a real business but to take it to the next level as an academic exercise. [48]

By then, Yang and Filo discovered that they worked well together. The more outgoing Yang with his interest in organizing business operations fit together well with the more inward, focused, technical Filo. They shared a common vision of exploring the Web and helping people find their way on-line.

Yahoo!

The two young entrepreneurs left Stanford to try to make some sort of business out of their Web guide. Filo concentrated on the programming, while Yang focused on figuring out a way to make some money from their site. Advertising on the net was still rare, and it seemed unlikely that people would be willing to pay to use the list. But perhaps this interesting, growing collection of information could be linked to the more commercial websites that were beginning to sell goods, services, and specialized information. The sites featured on the Web list would then pay a small fee based on how much business had been attracted.

In early 1995 Yang and Filo visited many venture capitalists—the people who offered money to promising startup companies in exchange for a share in their ownership. Yang, doing most of the talking, tried to convince them that companies would pay to be included on their list. They had little luck until they met Mike Moritz of Sequoia Capital, who had invested in many successful computer companies including Apple Computer, Atari, Cisco Systems, and Oracle. Moritz later described his visit to Yang and Filo's "headquarters," which resembled nothing more than college dorm rooms:

> [They] were sitting in this cube with the shades drawn tight, the Sun [Web] servers generating a ferocious amount of heat, the answering machine going on and off every couple of minutes, golf clubs stashed against the walls, pizza cartons on the floor, and unwashed clothes strewn around. It was every mother's idea of the bedroom she wished her sons never had. [49]

David Filo and Jerry Yang made their headquarters in a space that resembled a college dorm room.

Moritz might have been expected to turn down two grungy young men, barely out of their teens, who had yet to earn a dime and had no real business plan. But something about their attitude and spirit appealed to him. Part of that spirit is shown in the way they came up with a new, catchier name for their "Jerry and Dave" site. They had already decided that it should start with "Ya," Which stood for "Yet another" and was a reference to an obscure computer utility. However, they thought that using "Yang" for the name would be a bit too egotistical.

Yang recalls that when they came up with the name Yahoo! "the date is hazy, but it was definitely at two A.M." [50] They claimed that the name meant "Yet Another Hierarchic Officious Oracle." (The "hierarchic" meant that it was divided into different levels of topics, subtopics, and subsubtopics.) To Yang and Filo, Yahoo! expressed an energetic if irreverent delight in the possibilities of exploring the World Wide Web.

After seeing the number of hits to the site, Moritz decided to invest $1 million in the fledgling company. They then received word that the giant America Online was interested in taking over their guide service and would pay them quite well for it. Even though it was quite possible that AOL would start its own Web directory and become a formidable competitor, Yang and Filo agreed that they did not want to lose control over their creation. They went ahead with their plans.

Yang and Filo put their new money to work right away, hiring staff members, including Tim Koogle, who eventually became their president and CEO. They constantly expanded the site, adding more general and specific topics. For example, under "entertainment" would be found "amusement/theme parks" and many other subcategories. After going down enough levels, the user would then find actual website names, such as for particular amusement parks. Clicking on the site name takes the user directly to that site.

Unlike the robotic search engines, each of Yahoo!'s more than one hundred thousand categories and subtopics was put there by one of the company's hundreds of skilled Web surfers. Besides looking for new links and evaluating them to see whether they were interesting or useful enough to be listed, Yahoo!'s workers also had to check existing links and remove them when the site they pointed to no longer existed (a common occurrence on the rapidly changing Web).

Businessman Tim Koogle became the president and CEO of Yahoo! in 1995.

Commercial Links

While Filo focused on expanding the topics and links, Yang pursued his key idea of building relationships with other companies. He forged an alliance with Netscape, at the time the leading Web browser. In the new version of the Netscape browser, when a user clicked on the directory button, he or she would be taken to Yahoo!'s home page.

Yang also decided to allow companies to rent advertising space on the Yahoo! site. This decision was controversial. Many of the most outspoken Web users still came from the academic community and were suspicious about commercialism. But that particular battle was lost, and advertising became an integral part of the Web. Meanwhile, Yang and his colleagues decided that advertising could provide the income they needed to turn the former hobby into a self-sustaining business. In August 1995 Yahoo! sold advertising to five businesses, charging them $60,000 apiece for a three-month trial.

It became clear that information had the power to attract consumers who would then be exposed to advertisements and who would be potential customers for the many stores and services becoming available on the Web. Yahoo! began to snowball as it attracted more information providers to the site, including the Reuters news service, which created a link on Yahoo! that allowed users to read breaking news stories. Yahoo! soon added other news features such as weather reports, sports scores, and stock quotes.

Yang's vision for Yahoo! was not only about helping users find information and helping companies find customers on-line. He also believed that users would be more likely to stick with Yahoo! if they could personalize it by selecting what information would appear when they visited the site. Therefore, Yahoo! added a new feature that gave users the power to create "My Yahoo!" pages that reflected their interests. This encouraged users to make Yahoo! their home page—the first page they would see when starting their Web browser, and their jumping-off place to the many destinations the Web now had to offer. Yahoo! also pioneered using software to keep track of the Web pages users visited and using their interests to show them targeted ads. All these activities also served to make Yahoo! a valuable brand name that other companies paid to be associated with.

Expanding the Service

Although the public and corporate interest in Yahoo! was gratifying, Yang knew that the real test of whether Yahoo! could become a major business was yet to come. On April 12, 1996, Yahoo! offered its stock to the public for the first time. On the first day of trading, the price of a share rose from the starting price of $13 all the way to $43, settling

Brian Wilson, NASDAQ vice president of global sales, shakes hands with Jerry Yang after Yahoo! closed as the second-largest first day gain in NASDAQ history.

back to $33. This was the second-largest first day gain in the history of the NASDAQ stock exchange. By the end of that day, Yahoo! was worth $848 million, and Yang and Filo were multimillionaires. (Yang's stock alone was worth $132 million.)

Yahoo! continued to grow. Yang reached out to new groups of people. He created "Yahooligans!," a version of their directory designed for children, which offered special easy-to-use features and excluded adult material. Yahoo! also created Web directories in other languages including French, German, and Japanese. These new projects reflected Yang's continuing idea of the power of linking—linking ideas and linking people through their many diverse interests.

As the money began to roll in, they invested it in further expansion. They bought Geocities, a service that allows users to create their own free Web page. They helped the large retailer Kmart launch an on-line store. They planned to offer streamlined versions of their pages to users of handheld computers and even cell phones. By 1997 Yang exclaimed that "The level at which people are building up connectivity is growing by leaps and bounds. As a commercial medium, the Net hasn't yet been tapped." [51]

In less than six years, the two college students had transformed a simple directory of websites into one of the net's biggest success stories. They were attracting yearly revenues of $1 billion and the Yahoo! site received more than 190 million visitors from around the world each month. At its peak, on January 3, 2000, the company was worth $128 billion, more than twice the worth of media giant the Walt Disney Company.

Yahoo! Comes of Age

Like Marc Andreessen, the founder of Netscape, Jerry Yang had mixed feelings about his newfound wealth. He still dressed like a college student, but he bought a nice house in Los Altos, California. He told an interviewer that "I can honestly say that [Yahoo!'s success] hasn't changed my life at all, except that I think more about taxes." [52] Yang married his longtime girlfriend Akiko. (She keeps her maiden name private.)

Yang's combination of boundless energy and levelheadedness has contributed to his success. He commented to author Robert Reid that his relationship with his friend and business partner David Filo had al-

In less than six years, Jerry Yang and David Filo transformed their simple Web directory into one of the Internet's biggest success stories.

ways been strong and steady. "We've been through some rough times, [but] we've never had rough times together."[53]

Yang and Filo found that their own personalities were one of their most important assets. Their image is young, hip, and cool. As Robert Reid notes:

Their trailer-to-riches story is the stuff of legends. It is a familiar piece of Internet lore, and the company is not shy about retelling and promoting it. Jerry and Dave's PR [public relations] value has earned them coverage on countless TV shows and magazine covers (including those of *Wired* and *Forbes ASAP*). Through these channels, they can reach Yahoo! users off-line and reaffirm their company's youth, sense of humor, and up-from-the-trenches credibility.[54]

In 2000 Yahoo! celebrated its fifth birthday. When Yang was asked by an interviewer how he felt about his work, he admitted that he was still deeply immersed in it.

Yahoo! is such a big part of my life that I don't think of this as a job. When I'm here, it's one sort of frenetic pace, but when I'm on the road it's even worse. It's, like, gotta just be on all the time. I can't imagine doing anything else. We're at a stage where we're big enough to really make a lot of changes, to help people's lives on the Internet. But we're small enough that we can move fast, and we don't have to get bogged down in bureaucracy.[55]

Yang was then asked whether such a lifestyle, including rewards such as a big house felt unreal to him. He responded wryly, "Well, I wouldn't say it feels unreal, but I do have a feeling of quiet amazement sometimes when I think about what's happened. I mean, who would have predicted that Yahoo! would be where it is today? I'm like a kid in a candy store—except the candy store is the size of an airport."[56]

But 2000 brought some serious challenges to Yang and Yahoo!. Just as Marc Andreessen had to face a huge, powerful competitor in Microsoft, Yahoo! now faced new competition from aggressive America Online. AOL bought Time-Warner, a large conglomerate that owned many publishing, newspaper, and media companies. AOL could offer much more extensive news and other information content like that provided by Yahoo!'s associated links. Yang and CEO Tim Koogle debated whether they, too, should buy a media company and merge it into Yahoo! to strengthen their information content. In the end, however, they decided to continue with the more gradual, modest expansion that had brought them success before.

Yang and Yahoo! also considered buying the hugely successful on-line auction company eBay, which had been a proven steady revenue generator. But quarrels among Yahoo!'s executives about how they and eBay CEO Meg Whitman would work together in the merged company led to that merger's cancellation.

In the first quarter of 2001 Yahoo!'s revenues dropped by about half after steadily climbing since 1998. In April 2001 the company announced that because of falling ad sales, it would lay off four hundred employees and eliminate some services. Tim Koogle announced his resignation. The company shifted its focus from selling advertising to providing subscription information services to customers, such as real-time stock quotes. It also offered a fee-based on-line music store.

Along with other dot-coms, Yahoo! is now struggling to find new sources of revenue. But Yahoo! has $1.7 billion in the bank and is in a better position than most other on-line companies.

Finding Perspective

As Yahoo! grew, Yang's role in the company changed. The company is now too large for him to be involved in all of its day-to-day operations. Yahoo! has skilled executives and managers to continue developing Yang's vision.

John Hennessy, provost of Stanford University, notes that

> It's a real challenge for companies and entrepreneurs when the founders don't find a meaningful role. The entire company suffers . . . [but] Jerry has managed to sculpt out a new kind of role for a founder that is as important as Koogle's or anybody else's at Yahoo: He's everything from technical visionary to chief strategist to corporate spokesman and cheerleader to Washington lobbyist to the company's conscience. [57]

Yang believes that business is only one important facet of his life. He has kept his career in perspective by stressing the importance of family and enduring values:

> My family is very close. My brother and I still go home every Sunday to Mom. She cooks dinner. And she packs it up for us to take for the rest of the week. I think that a lot of people who meet me say I'm basically a normal guy. I am. I don't know how else to be other than who I am. Hopefully, no amount of money or fame will change that. It's unfortunate that people do change because of external circumstances. If I want to change, it should be an intrinsic change. [58]

Whatever happens in the future, Jerry Yang has already made history as one of the most successful early Internet pioneers. He achieved his success through seeing that the power of the Web lay not just in connecting machines, but also in connecting people to information and, through their interests, to one another. In building Yahoo!, he made his own personal links to other entrepreneurs as well as to investors, convincing them that they could have mutually profitable arrangements. It is such links that are creating a new economy and perhaps a new society.

CHAPTER 6

Jeff Bezos: The World's Biggest Bookstore

The world of computers seems to be filled with the unreal and intangible: words, images, numbers passing through wires and lighting up screens. Many of the Internet pioneers made their careers from software and data. However, even though this era is often called the Information Revolution, much of the world's economy involves the selling of actual, physical goods such as books. Amazon founder Jeff Bezos added a new chapter to the story of Internet commerce by proving that one could indeed sell large quantities of goods on the Web. In doing so, he changed the world of retailing just as F. W. Woolworth did with his five-and-dime stores, and Sears and Montgomery Ward did with their mail-order catalogs a century ago.

To succeed, Bezos adapted the traditional ways of distributing and selling books to a system where users could browse for and select books and other items on-line. Like other Internet pioneers, Bezos used imagination and vision. But Bezos was also a practical business leader. Like a successful football coach, he learned to master the details of complex business "plays" and inspire his team to execute them. In doing so, he has become an example of leadership in the new economy of the Internet.

The Infinity Cube

Jeff Bezos was born on January 12, 1964, and he grew up in Miami, Florida. Shortly after Jeff's birth, his mother, Jacklyn Gise (pronounced "Gice"), remarried, so he grew up with his stepfather, Miguel Bezos. At age fifteen, Miguel Bezos fled Cuba. (The name Bezos is pronounced BAY-zohs and means "kisses.")

Growing up, Jeff demonstrated that he was a strong-willed child. When he was three he decided that he wanted a "grownup" bed, but his mother thought he was too young to leave the crib. Jeff found a screwdriver and began to dismantle the crib to try to build a bed. In preschool, Jeff became so absorbed in whatever he happened to be doing that his teachers had to pick him and his chair up and move them to the next activity.

As he grew older, Jeff became fascinated with electronic gadgets. He saw an "Infinity Cube," a gadget with motorized mirrors that created "infinite" reflections within reflections. His mother would not pay $20 for one, so Jeff figured out what parts were needed, bought them separately at Radio Shack (they were cheaper than the whole device), and built his own Infinity Cube.

Jeff did not limit his interests to electronics, however. Despite his relatively small size, Jeff played Youth League football, and his coach was so impressed by his determination that he made him captain of the team.

Another important time for Jeff was the summers he spent at the Texas ranch of his grandfather Preston Gise, who was manager of the regional office of the Atomic Energy Commission. Previously, his grandfather had worked for DARPA, the agency that developed what would become the Internet in the 1970s. He gave Jeff many gadgets to take home and play with. His mother remembers that "there was always something going on in our garage. His projects became more complex with age but unfortunately the garage never got any bigger." [59]

Amazon.com founder Jeff Bezos changed the world of Internet commerce with the development of a company that could sell large quantities of books via the Web.

He was also introduced to ranch chores such as branding and vaccinating cattle. Jeff's high school girlfriend Ursula Werner believes that Jeff's grandfather played an important part in shaping his character: "Jeff would speak of his grandfather with great love. . . . It made me realize what a profound bond there must have been between them. I got the sense that he gave Jeff a lot of freedom, which is what grandparents do, and encouraged Jeff to be who he ultimately has become." [60]

"New Ways of Thinking"

Jeff's varied experience and wide-ranging interests continued during his years at Palmetto High School. He became fascinated by the possibilities of space travel and the future of humankind among the stars. He dreamed of becoming an astronaut or, failing that, a physicist. He won

Jeff Bezos graduated summa cum laude from Princeton University.

a trip to NASA's Marshall Spaceflight Center in Huntsville, Alabama, for writing a paper entitled "The Effect of Zero Gravity on the Aging Rate of the Common Housefly." He spent much time thinking about how space stations and colonies might be used to move people and industry into space. He felt that "the whole idea was to preserve the Earth . . . to get all the people off the Earth and see it turned into a huge national park." [61]

Jeff may have had his eyes on the stars, but he continued to work hard at his studies. Several times he won the annual awards for Best Science Student and Best Math Student. In 1982 Jeff graduated from high school as the first out of 680 students and was made valedictorian.

Jeff was not too serious to have fun, however. He had a good sense of humor and was outgoing and generous toward his friends. For Ursula's eighteenth birthday, he created an elaborate treasure hunt with many clever clues. Jeff and Ursula also created and ran a small educational summer camp. The camp's program brought together science and literature (particularly science fiction and fantasy) and emphasized what his camp flyer called "the use of new ways of thinking in old areas." [62] The ability to think about new ways to do things helped him when he created Amazon.com.

In 1982 Bezos entered Princeton University. He studied physics, but despite doing well, he decided that he could not reach true genius. "It was really sort of a startling insight, that there were those people whose brains were wired differently." [63] This insight also reflected the very high standards that Bezos set for himself: Doing merely well was not enough. Nevertheless, in 1986 he graduated summa cum laude (with greatest honors) with a degree in electrical engineering and computer science. As evidence of his being ready to meet any future challenge, his college yearbook photo is accompanied by a line from science fiction writer Ray Bradbury: "The Universe says No to us. We in answer fire a broadside of flesh at it and cry Yes!" [64]

Launching a Business Career

In 1986 Bezos was hired for his first real job in the business world. He worked as a software engineer for Fitel, a company involved with financial communications—wiring of transactions and information between the world's markets. His first challenge was building a new financial network called Equinet. He managed the efforts of twelve programmers and commuted between the company's New York and London offices every week. After looking at the company's trading practices, Bezos was able to make changes that cut expenses by 30 percent. At only twenty-three years old, Bezos showed impressive technical, financial, and management skills. He had also received a crash course in what would eventually be called "electronic commerce"—the buying and selling of goods and services over computer networks.

Bezos's career continued to advance rapidly. In 1988 he moved to Bankers Trust Company, a major Wall Street investment firm. He became the youngest vice president in its history. In charge of global fiduciary [money management] services, he was responsible for pension and profit-sharing plans for more than five hundred of America's top companies, totaling more than $250 billion in assets.

In this position, Bezos constantly looked for ways to put new technology to work to increase productivity. For example, he wanted people to obtain investment information immediately through on-line terminals. But he encountered resistance. As Harvey Hirsch, for whom Bezos worked at the time, recalled, "This was something that couldn't be done, shouldn't be done, and that the traditional way of delivering information in hard copy was better. . . . The feeling was: Why change? Why make the investment?"[65]

But once Bezos was convinced that something could be done in a better way, he was persistent. As Hirsch recalled:

> Jeff has a way of stripping away the extraneous and focusing on what's really important. He sees different ways of doing things and better ways of doing things. He told the naysayers, "I believe in this new technology and I'm going to show you how it's going to work."—and he did. At the end of the day, he proved them all wrong. He has no trouble puncturing someone's balloon if he thinks that they're proposing to do something the wrong way or in an inappropriate way. He'll argue his point of view very persuasively. That doesn't mean that he didn't break some eggs in the process because he proved people wrong, but I don't think he ever did it in a way that angered or infuriated people. It was all very professional.[66]

Another admiring colleague, Halsey Minor of Merrill Lynch, believes that "Outside of Bill Gates, I think there are few other people who share Jeff's deep technical understanding and combine it with highly refined strategic and tactical instincts."[67]

E-Commerce Insights

By 1990, however, Bezos was getting restless. He mastered the world of electronic finance, but he believed that what he had been doing was just the first phase of a business revolution that would make on-line purchasing a part of everyday life. It was unclear just how this was going to happen. However, his boss at the D. E. Shaw Company then asked him to look into possible Internet business opportunities.

Bezos soon discovered that Internet use was growing at an astounding 2,300 percent a year. As a potential market, the net was becoming quite attractive. The problem was deciding what could be practically (and profitably) sold on-line. After doing some research and analyzing, Bezos compiled a list of twenty possible products, including computer software, office supplies, clothing, music—and books.

Even without the Internet, the book industry was rapidly changing, with big chains such as Barnes & Noble, Borders, and the discount bookseller Crown Books using high volume and low prices to take market share away from traditional bookstores. Yet Bezos felt that an opportunity existed for using the technology of the Internet to outsell the chains. More than 3 million different books were in print from

Bezos could offer more titles than a regular bookstore could afford to stock by combining a huge database of books with a highly automated ordering system.

thousands of publishers. Barnes & Noble and Borders together accounted for only about 25 percent of the market. The limited shelf and warehouse space of even the biggest chains simply did not allow them to efficiently stock obscure or hard-to-find titles.

By combining a huge database of books with a highly automated ordering system, Bezos could offer far more titles than the regular bookstores could afford to stock. By enabling customers to browse and learn about books and order them immediately on-line, he could eliminate the cost of retail stores stocking their shelves and paying clerks to manually ring up purchases.

Bezos asked D. E. Shaw to back an on-line book business, but the firm decided it was not a solid enough investment. When Bezos said that he was thinking of starting an on-line book business on his own, Shaw himself tried to persuade his talented executive not to leave, telling him he was on a fast track to becoming a top executive. Bezos thought about it for two days. In the end, he decided that he could not pass up what was likely to be a fleeting opportunity.

I knew that when I was eighty there was no chance I would regret having walked away from my 1994 Wall Street bonus in the middle of the year. I wouldn't even have *remembered* that. But I did think there was a chance I might regret significantly not participating in this thing called the Internet, that I believe passionately in. I also knew that if I tried and failed, I wouldn't regret that. So once I thought about it that way, it became incredibly easy to make that decision.[68]

A Very Big River

Bezos decided to leave Shaw and start an on-line bookselling business. He first needed a headquarters and a name. He wanted to set up his headquarters in an area that had a good supply of technically trained people. He also wanted it to be located in a state with a small population, because only the customers in the same state as the store would have to pay sales tax. He considered Portland, Oregon; Boulder, Colorado; Lake Tahoe, Nevada; and Seattle, Washington. He eventually decided on Seattle.

After several ideas and some debate, Bezos decided to call his company Amazon. Later, he explained his reasoning: "Earth's biggest river, Earth's biggest bookstore. The Amazon River is 10 times as large as the next largest river, which is the Mississippi, in terms of volume of water. Twenty percent of the world's fresh water is in the Amazon River Basin, and we have six times as many titles as the world's largest physical bookstore."[69]

Bezos then threw himself into learning both the technology needed for managing a large store and the basics of the bookselling business in particular. He hired Sheldon Kaphan, a programmer with a stellar reputation for setting up database systems. Bezos also took a course from the American Booksellers Association for new bookstore owners. One of his fellow students at the ABA remembers that "When students were asked their plans . . . here was this kind of cute, dorky guy who stood up and said, 'I'm going to start an Internet bookstore.' The room fell silent. I'm sure half the people were confused and the other half was thinking, 'Yeah, a computer geek. Whatever.'"[70]

In November 1994 Bezos, his wife Mackenzie, and a handful of employees set up Amazon.com in a converted garage. Bezos decided that the existing software for running a mail-order business was too limited in its ability to track purchases and shipments. Bezos wanted to track books according to when they would be available, with seven categories ranging from "shipped within 24 hours" to "out of print, shipped within 1 to 3 months if it can be found." Most mail-order businesses were content to have one or two such categories. As a colleague recalled, "Jeff insisted on a business model that was going to work for us, not a business model that was built into some other software. . . . Jeff's insistence was on everything being done right."[71] He closely worked with chief programmer Shel Kaphan to make sure the software would meet their needs.

Through early 1995 they rushed to finish the ordering system. They encouraged friends to place fake orders so they could test the software. Because Bezos knew that many potential on-line purchasers were concerned about the safety of their credit card information, Amazon.com set up a completely separate computer to hold the credit card details. When an order arrived, Bezos or one of his assistants saved the incoming data to a floppy and then walked over to the credit card processing computer and inserted the disk. This ensured that hackers breaking into his main computer would not be able to access customers' credit card numbers.

A Trickle, Then a Flood

Once they were ready to go on-line, they packed up all the equipment in the garage and installed it in a Seattle office. Financing for the first months of operations was provided by Jeff's mother, who invested $145,553 from the family trust. They waited to see when the first order would come in. As Bezos recalls, "It is very exciting when you get your first customer who is not a relative. . . . All the staff were saying 'Do you know this person? I don't know this person. Hey, how about you? Do you know this person?'"[72]

First the orders trickled in; then came the flood. Three days after they opened, another new Internet company, Jerry Yang and David Filo's Yahoo!, sent Bezos an e-mail asking him whether they could include a link to Amazon on their site. Bezos wryly notes that

> Today, to get Yahoo! to do something like that, you'd have to pay them ten million dollars. Then, it was just an e-mail exchange. So, we sat around, seven or nine of us, eating Chinese food, discussing whether or not we were ready for what Shel Kaphan said "might be like taking a sip through a fire hose." We talked about it for five minutes and said, "Yeah, let's do it."[73]

Aided by the Yahoo! listing and recommendations in on-line chat rooms and news forums, customers began to order in droves. The first week Amazon.com took $12,438 in orders but could only ship $846 worth of books because they had not built up their inventory yet. The next week, they took in $14,792 and shipped $7,302 worth of books.

Bezos believed that providing good information about books would be a key to drawing people in to shop there. Each worker in the Amazon.com office was assigned to read ten books a week and write a review to be posted with the book's listing. The staff also kept track of the oddest book titles ordered each week. Examples include *Training Goldfish Using Dolphin Training Techniques, How to Start Your Own Country,* and *Life Without Friends.*

Making the Pitch

Although Amazon.com was attracting considerable interest and had little real competition from other on-line bookstores, expenses ran well ahead of profit from orders. By summer 1995 the company was heading for a loss of $303,000. By then Bezos was broke and his family could offer him no further funds. He believed, however, that if the idea was sound, profits would come eventually. He was willing to wait five years to become profitable—unprecedented in the modern business world. But he would have to find venture capitalists willing to invest in his company.

Bezos was good at selling ideas to colleagues, but he was not yet good at selling *himself.* Yet one investor, Eric Dillon, who also had a background on Wall Street, was fascinated by Bezos and his company. Because Bezos had given up a Wall Street job worth more than $1 million a year to start his business, Dillon believed that Bezos believed in himself. Bezos explained to Dillon and investors how technology would give him the edge against traditional bookstores:

> You could build a bookstore on the Web that simply couldn't exist any other way. The Web is an infant technology. If you want to be successful in the short-to-medium term, you can only do things that offer incredibly strong value propositions to customers relative to the value of doing things in more traditional ways. That basically means that, right now, you should only do online what you cannot do any other way. [74]

The leverage that could bring Amazon.com large profits came from several sources. Part of the secret was cash flow, or how fast the company could get money for its books. A traditional bookstore had to pay its book supplier in less than 90 days, but the average book sat on the shelf for 160 days before it was sold and the store got its money. At Amazon, however, information about the demand for books was continually being fed into the ordering system. Thus, Amazon's warehouse was much more efficiently stocked, and the average book waited only 18 days before being sold. Amazon could thus get paid by the customer and use the customer's money for more than 50 days before the supplier had to be paid for the book.

Because information about the demand for books was continually being fed into the ordering system, Amazon.com could get money for its books more quickly.

Bezos managed to net almost $1 million in new funding to keep the company afloat. At the same time, he was worried. Looking back with a bit of humor he recalls that "I told all our early investors that we would lose their money for sure. I think this is a good technique when you're taking money from friends and family because you still want to be able to go to Thanksgiving dinner." [75]

Bezos's uncertainty about the future could have made him more cautious, but it did not. He believed that e-commerce was growing exponentially, and that it would be a mistake to try to keep just the products and services he was offering and concentrate on being profitable. Instead, his motto, as printed on company T-shirts, was "Get Big Fast." Getting big meant competing to offer many different goods and services, not just books. If Amazon.com could become the dominant company in many areas, with the biggest market share (portion of customers), then as e-commerce grew, Amazon.com would be in a position to finally rake in huge profits.

Focusing on Customer Service

In carrying out his growth strategy, Bezos focused on expanding the product line and expanding customer service. Just as Jerry Yang's Yahoo! used the ability to link users to information to attract visitors to his site, Bezos tied together products with related information. He believed that eventually Amazon.com would be able to offer its customers a complete information service that would enable them to find and buy just about anything they needed. He states:

> In the future, when you come to Amazon.com, I don't want you just to be able to search for *kayak* and find all the books on kayaking. You should also be able to read articles on kayaking and buy subscriptions to kayaking magazines. You should be able to buy a kayaking trip to anywhere in the world you want to go kayaking, and you should be able to have a kayak delivered to your house. You should be able to discuss kayaking with other kayakers. There should be everything to do with kayaking, and the same should be true for anything.[76]

Besides selling through an interconnected web of information, Amazon.com added other products such as music CDs and electronic equipment. It developed a network with used book dealers so customers could order out-of-print books. It even added an auction section, although it remains overshadowed by the giant eBay.

Using technology to improve customer service has also been a consistent theme for Amazon. Once a user has browsed and shopped the Amazon site, the software keeps track of the kinds of books or other goods the user has been looking at. The site then starts producing customized recommendations of other books that are likely to be of interest to that user. Users are also encouraged to discuss books and add book reviews to the book listings. Amazon's technology is designed to allow customers to serve' as additional salespersons by letting people know what other people are reading and recommending.

Profitable or Not?

By 1997 Bezos headed a company that was rapidly growing and had become a dominant player in e-commerce. On May 15 of that year Amazon.com made its first public stock offering at $18 per share. The stock price rose to $30, then tumbled below the offering price of $18. But a year later the stock was worth almost $100 a share, and by 1999 Jeff Bezos' personal wealth was around $7.5 billion. In October 1997, Amazon celebrated its one millionth customer, a Japanese consumer who ordered a Windows NT book and a biography of Princess Diana. Bezos flew to Japan to personally deliver the books.

With continuous growth Amazon is not only the world's largest bookstore, but also the world's largest on-line store. However, in 2000 its stock declined about 30 percent as investors began to question whether the company would ever become profitable. Bezos claims not to be worried:

In early 1996 we were called Amazon.con, in '97 Amazon.toast, and in 1999 it was Amazon.bomb. Then there was my personal favorite—Amazon.org, because clearly we're not for profit. But e-commerce is still a rapidly growing, important segment of the future economy. It still gets a ton of attention. I mean, you're still talking to me. [77]

But as of early 2001, Amazon is still losing money (despite sales of $695 million for the first quarter). Bezos believes the company is still on track to becoming profitable by the fourth quarter. However that will depend on many factors, including whether the economy recovers from its current downturn. Meanwhile, with investors becoming more demanding, Bezos has begun to shift some of his emphasis from growth to profitability. He believes that by offering a large selection

Some of the many offerings that help Amazon survive and grow are the wide variety of books stocked.

and wide variety of goods, having the ability to sell hard-to-find goods with a high profit margin, and continuing to fine-tune its inventory system, Amazon.com will survive and grow. However, he admitted to an interviewer that the road has become a bumpy one. "The last year, I think, has been a brutal one in every way. . . . In one year, it's easy to go from being Internet poster boy to Internet piñata." [78]

Bezos applied the classic principles of business management and marketing to use the new technology of the Web to sell not only information, but also physical goods. But he also demonstrated the value of being focused and disciplined in the face of the challenges of a changing economy. As his ideas continue to be tested by the demands of the marketplace, he reshapes and adapts them.

CHAPTER 7

Pierre Omidyar: Commerce Through Community

Suppose a family has a garage full of "stuff" that they decide they no longer need. Perhaps that pile of stuff includes a model car kit from the 1950s in its original box, or a set of ornamental bookends, and grandpa's old stamp collection. Whatever the items might be, the family could bring them to a hobby shop or antique store and see what price a dealer might offer for the goods. Or they might have a garage sale and hope that someone passing by might show some interest in one or more of the objects.

Today there is another way in which millions of people are buying and selling their possessions. A website called eBay has thousands of different kinds of merchandise. For a small fee, anyone can list an item for auction, and the site's millions of visitors can use the search engine to find and browse for whatever interests them.

In creating eBay, young Pierre Omidyar would pioneer a different kind of e-commerce. Instead of selling goods to customers from a central location (as Amazon.com and other on-line stores do), eBay brings together buyers and sellers who carry out their transactions directly with one another. In creating eBay, Omidyar saw that the Web was not just an information system. It was also a *social* system: a new way for people to relate to one another. He believed that people could, by and large, be trusted to deal fairly with each other using this new medium. He remained focused on his concern about ethics and social relationships as eBay grew and faced a variety of challenges.

Coming to America

Pierre Omidyar was born in Paris on June 27, 1967, but at age six his family came to America and he grew up near Washington, D.C. His family is of Iranian descent, and the name Omidyar means "he who has hope on his side" in Iran's Farsi language. His father, a doctor, accepted a residency at Johns Hopkins University Medical Center. However, his parents divorced, although they remained near each other so the boy could spend time with both of them.

In high school Pierre became intrigued with computer programming. Working for the school library for $6 per hour, he wrote a program to catalog its books. He became what he later described as a "typical nerd or geek," [79] sneaking out of gym class so he could spend more time programming.

After graduation Omidyar went to Tufts University and majored in computer science. However, in his junior year he left school and went to Silicon Valley to help design a drawing program for the Macintosh. After a year, he went back to school and finished his degree in 1988. He then went back to the valley to work for Claris, a subsidiary of Apple Computer. There he helped develop MacDraw, a popular graphics application for the Macintosh.

By 1991 Omidyar became interested in finding new ways for people to use computers to store and communicate information. He and three partners started their own company, Ink Development. The company developed an electronic pen intended to let people input data in their own handwriting. This technology was useful for people who had to record information while they were on the move—people such as delivery drivers or nurses, for example. But the "pen computing" market turned out to be rather limited. The company changed its focus (and name) and became eShop, specializing in e-commerce, including

Meg Whitman and Pierre Omidyar leaf through an eBay catalog. Omidyar created eBay, an on-line auction that brings buyers and sellers together.

order-taking systems for on-line businesses. Later, Omidyar also worked as a programmer for General Magic, a company specializing in graphics and special effects for movies.

A Different Kind of E-Commerce

While many Internet pioneers had misgivings about the commercialization of the Web, Omidyar took a different approach. He believed in a business philosophy that stressed empowering individuals by giving them the freedom to create new social arrangements to suit their needs. Omidyar later explained how he tried to apply this philosophy to the on-line world of the Web.

Now linking millions of buyers and sellers together, eBay began as a way for individuals to trade Pez candy dispensers.

Being a software engineer by training, I was interested in doing interesting things and learning about new tools. That's how I got into the Web.... I also wanted to create an environment where individuals could benefit from the Internet. The businesses that were trying to come onto the Internet were trying to use the Internet to sell products to people—basically, the more people, the more stuff that could be sold. Coming from a democratic, libertarian point of view, I didn't think that was such a great idea, having corporations just cram more products down people's throats. I wanted to give the individual the power to be a producer as well. [80]

As he began to explore the possibilities of Web commerce, his fiancée, Pam, a management consultant, asked him whether they could use a website to help collectors trade Pez, a candy dispenser that comes in many interesting designs. Using Web software that he had mastered, he built a site called AuctionWeb that could run simple auctions online. Omidyar's site started out simple but grew more extensive as he added more categories of collectibles to the site. Soon a growing stream of sellers and bidders were using his service, which started out as a free service.

However, as the traffic increased, Omidyar's Internet Service Provider (ISP) raised his monthly bill from $30 to $250. So he then decided to charge sellers a nominal fee of $.10 per item listed, plus a few percent of the value of each item sold. He was soon getting a thousand visits or "hits" a day, and the stream of small checks coming in the mail started to add up—$250 the first month, then $1,000, $2,000, $5,000, and $10,000. Omidyar recalls that "I really started [what became] eBay not as a company, but as a hobby. It wasn't until I was nine months into it that I realized I was making more money from my hobby than [from] my day job." [81]

From Hobby to Business

The growing demand for his auction service convinced Omidyar that he should make it his full-time job. If he could get money from investors, he could create a major company. But the prospects of finding investment capital to expand his business did not seem very good. "I remember saying that if we went in the beginning to venture capitalists or to business analysts and told them about the kind of business we were starting, they would have laughed at us," Omidyar recalls. [82] "E-commerce" and "dot-com" were not yet industry buzzwords.

However, his need for more money was about to be met from an unexpected source. Microsoft bought his former company eShop, paying Omidyar $1 million for his share in the company. He recalls how incredulous he felt at that turn of events. "You get a million dollars? When you're twenty-nine? Hey, take some time off. Take a *lot* of time off." [83]

But Omidyar was interested in making things happen, not just sitting around and enjoying his windfall. He quit his job at General Magic and made his auction site his full-time business. He believed that on-line auctions would succeed because they tapped into a powerful economic idea: "I'd always been interested in financial markets just generally, and I've been attracted by the theory that in an efficient market, goods trade at their true value." [84]

Omidyar knew that the auction process itself was an efficient market because the price at the end of an auction represents the highest price someone is willing to pay for an item. With his AuctionWeb site, Omidyar essentially kept the auction and threw out the auction house and its costs and fees. Now a seller could post baseball cards or Beanie

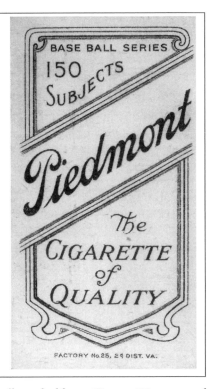

EBay allowed sellers to post baseball cards like a Honus Wagner card estimated to sell for more than $1 million on eBay.

Babies in the appropriate auction category, and interested bidders could use a list of topics and a search engine to find the item and bid on it. After a specified period such as five days, the person with the highest bid and the seller would exchange e-mail and make arrangements for payment and shipment of the item. The auction site would collect only a small fee. However, as the number of auctions grew week by week, so did the total of those small payments.

But on-line auctions turned out to be more than a business. People often continued to communicate with one another and make friends even after a transaction was completed. Omidyar became enthusiastic about the potential community growing up around his service. Omidyar began to look for a business partner and he found a reliable partner in Jeff Skoll, a Canadian-born engineer who had started two small businesses of his own while studying for his master's at Stanford. Omidyar and Skoll worked well together in planning the future of the business. Skoll noted that "[Omidyar's] a very cerebral [thinking] guy. His finest attribute is that he's always able to ask the right questions.

If there's something he knows nothing about, he manages to come up with the three or four questions that get to the very heart of what he's trying to find out." [85] Omidyar in turn found that Skoll could focus intensely and apply his analytical skills to deal with the many practical problems involved in expanding the auction site, which was renamed eBay (a combination of the "e" in "electronic" and the San Francisco Bay area where they lived).

Growing Profits and Growing Pains

By 1996 many e-businesses were starting, but eBay was unusual in one important way. Most companies, even the rapidly growing Amazon.com, were not actually making a profit. Some entrepreneurs such as Jeff Bezos of Amazon.com had made a conscious decision to pour all revenues back into the business to pay for further expansion. EBay, however, made money from the first day of business, and kept making more and more as people discovered the site.

Omidyar and Skoll thought about making more money by selling their auction software to other people who might want to start their own auction sites. While such sales could bring in a lot of money, they would also be helping set up their own future competition. Instead, the partners decided to stick with their core auction business but seek some capital for further expansion. They found a venture capital firm called Benchmark.

In their first meeting with Benchmark, Omidyar and Skoll ran into a common example of "Murphy's Law"—the tendency of things to go wrong at the worst possible time. Trying to demonstrate their auction system, they attempted to log into eBay from Benchmark's office, only to find that eBay had crashed. However, the people at Benchmark were patient, and it also happened that one of their partners collected fishing lures. When the eBay server came back up, he began to browse the listings and soon became "hooked." Benchmark decided to give eBay the money they needed.

Besides funding, eBay gained another important benefit from their relationship with Benchmark. Omidyar and Skoll met and hired Meg Whitman, an experienced executive and consultant.

At first Whitman was not impressed by the rather cluttered and messy eBay website. But when she explored further she saw both the wide range of products offered by eBay and the sheer enthusiasm of users posting on the site's feedback section. When she toured eBay's office, she saw a company that had very low overhead—no warehouse, no shipping costs and thus a very high profit margin. After a campaign of persuasion on the part of Omidyar, Skoll, and the Benchmark people, she signed on as eBay's vice president of marketing. Having an executive with Whitman's proven experience gave eBay more credibility with investors and potential business partners. As in joining with Skoll, Omidyar showed that he had a knack for building the kind of strong relations that are so important to a smooth-running business.

Toward the end of 1998 eBay prepared to put its stock on the market. Goldman-Sachs and the other bankers who had agreed to underwrite the stock offer became nervous after the Dow Jones average dropped several hundred points. But Omidyar and Skoll, now backed up by Whitman, continued to make the case for eBay to investors. In particular, Whitman explained to potential investors the strengths of eBay that led her to leave "a six-hundred million dollar division, managing some of the great brands in the world, to come to eBay." [86]

Meg Whitman holds up a promotional truck in her eBay office, where she works as chief executive officer.

Through all the meetings, Omidyar kept his quiet sense of humor and a perspective on the difference between his people-oriented way of doing business and the attitudes of the traditional Wall Street bigwigs. Later, he sketched this scene:

> I put a penny down on the carpet, wondering if any of the portfolio managers would stoop down to pick it up. Nah. I guess "a penny saved is a penny earned" doesn't jive with "I make more money on the stock market in the time it would take me to pick up a penny off the floor than most small countries make all year." Oh well. [87]

Hitting the Big Time

Finally the big day came. Omidyar and his colleagues waited to see what price their stock would reach. But when trading opened, the enthusiasm for eBay was so great that no one who had received the first batch of shares seemed willing to sell, even at a profit. Finally, when the price reached $54, some sales began. Meanwhile, according to writer Randall Stross, "Down in San Jose, eBay employees abandoned their cubicles and formed a giant conga line, a snake of conjoined, singing delirious adults that wound through an ordinary-looking office in an ordinary smallish office building in an ordinary-looking business park." [88]

As a result of the demand for eBay's stock, Omidyar, Whitman, and the other main people in eBay were now "paper millionaires," with $750 million for Omidyar alone. The price closed at $47, the fifth-highest first-day gain in the market's history.

Going into 1999 eBay grew steadily even as many other e-businesses seemed to falter as they failed to make enough profits to satisfy investors. But Omidyar and his colleagues would soon be tested in several different ways. First, competition arrived as other companies, including Yahoo! and Amazon.com, launched their own auction services.

Then, in June 1999, a flaw in the operating system that controlled eBay's servers caused the database to "crash," making the auction listings unavailable for several days. Omidyar posted a message on the site apologizing for the problems and assuring customers that eBay was installing a backup system that would minimize any future outages. With eBay temporarily down, Yahoo!'s auction listings rose from 250,000 to more than 400,000. After Omidyar warned investors that it was likely to actually lose $3 million to $5 million because of the outage, its stock began to slide until it had lost about 25 percent of its value.

However, eBay recovered from the crash. The loyalty of the community Omidyar had built proved to be its hidden asset. Three months later, listings had nearly doubled to 4.1 million. In 1999 eBay made

Going into 1999, Meg Whitman could safely open the doors of the steadily growing eBay headquarters, even when most e-businesses seemed to falter.

$10.8 million in profits on $224 million in revenues. As of early 2000 the site had about 10 million users, with more than 4 million items for sale at any one time, in more than three thousand categories. Among the millions of eBay users, a considerable number have created part-time or even full-time businesses buying and selling goods on-line. Even stamp, coin, and other collectibles dealers with their own shops have found that they cannot ignore eBay—and often can make money using it for certain items.

Building Community

If eBay's profitability and growth came from exploiting the economic factors that made on-line auctions work so well, its survival and continued health owe much to a second insight. Omidyar discovered the value of the long-term loyalty that comes from turning customers into a community. Omidyar says that he starts with what he learned in childhood from his mother, who "always taught me to treat other people the way I want to be treated and to have respect for other people. Those are just good basic values to have in a crowded world." [89]

Many people wondered why one stranger would trust another enough to send money for an item with no real assurance of receiving it. One reason is that while in many cases people in Internet chat rooms are anonymous, people on eBay have a verified identity. Further, there is an area on eBay where either party to a transaction can post comments about that transaction, including whether they feel they were treated fairly by the other party. As Omidyar explains, "We encourage people to give feedback to one another. People are concerned about their own reputations, and they are very easily able to evaluate other people's reputations. So it turns out that people kind of behave more like real people and less like strangers." [90]

According to Omidyar, the numbers show that his faith in building a community from feedback works: "I'm very proud of the fact that eBay has shown it to be true that 99 percent of the people are honest and trustworthy. My premise has held true. Otherwise eBay would not be trading $10 million a day between members." [91]

Of course not everyone is honest. A small number of sellers misrepresent the items they sell. There is the occasional well-publicized case of an expensive, fake item such as a Diebenkorn painting being offered on eBay. Occasionally someone takes the money for an item but fails to deliver it. The service has been criticized for not protecting people enough against such fraud.

Omidyar believes that he has worked hard to reduce the number of problems with auctions. EBay does insure small transactions and offers an escrow service, where the buyer's money is held until the item is delivered.

EBay is now a global service with buyers and sellers in many countries. In trying to extend his vision of a trustworthy on-line community into a world of diverse cultures, Omidyar has had to deal with criticisms from certain countries. Germany, for example, bans Nazi-related medals, uniforms, and similar paraphernalia. In response, Omidyar decided to ban all items relating to hate groups.

Burden or Opportunity?

In addition to business challenges, Omidyar also faces personal challenges and paradoxes. As a person who deeply loves his privacy, he has become something of a celebrity despite himself. He is often prominently featured in magazine lists of top net entrepreneurs. One writer described him as "the . . . King of Stuff [who] created an ingenious mechanism for mining value out of our cluttered, stuff-filled lives, a 'place' where groping buyers and latent sellers could meet and make order (and a few bucks) out of chaos." [92]

Yet Omidyar does not really collect much "stuff" himself. Nor is he that comfortable with the idea of being rich:

I've never been the kind of person who is comfortable with displays of wealth. . . . I will say that we have more money now than we ever wanted. So the bottom line is—well, you can't really talk about it in a way that's believable. But it's more of a burden than anything else. It's a burden that my wife and I are taking on very constructively, in that we have to find a good use for this wealth. [93]

Omidyar and his wife Pam have established a foundation that invests money to improve society. With the same commitment and energy with which he built eBay, Omidyar plans on giving away most of the wealth it has generated for him. So far the eBay Foundation has focused on giving neighborhood education groups money, computers, and the training they need to use them effectively.

Meanwhile, Omidyar and his wife have moved to his birthplace, Paris, where they live in a modest home. Although he now leaves the detailed operation of the company to its executives, Omidyar uses his laptop to stay in touch with eBay and who knows—perhaps he bids once in a while on another Pez dispenser for his wife's collection.

Pierre Omidyar became one of the most successful Internet pioneers because he was able to harness people's age-old desire to bargain and trade by building a system that would, by and large, allow them to do so safely and efficiently. By recognizing that social organization was just as important in the on-line world as technical skill, Omidyar has helped turn the advancing Communications and Information Revolutions into a social one as well. That revolution will continue as new Internet pioneers try to find and tap into the human need to both cooperate and to compete.

Notes

Chapter 1: Two Revolutions

1. Nathaniel Hawthorne, *The House of the Seven Gables.* Text available on-line at http://eldred.ne.mediaone.net/nh/sg.html.

2. Internet Society. "A Brief History of the Internet." Available on-line at www.isoc.org/internet/history/brief.html.

3. Leonard Kleinrock, "Information Flow in Large Communication Nets." [Ph.D. Thesis Proposal] Available on-line at www.lk.cs.ucla.edu/LK/Bib/REPORT/PhD.

4. Quoted in Howard Rheingold, *The Virtual Community: Homesteading on the Electronic Frontier.* Reading, MA: Addison-Wesley, 1993, p. 75.

5. Quoted in Stephen Segaller, *Nerds 2.0.1: A Brief History of the Internet.* New York: TV Books, 1999, pp. 92–93.

Chapter 2: Vinton Cerf: Building the Internet

6. Quoted in Elizabeth A. Schick, ed., *Current Biography Yearbook 1998.* New York: H. W. Wilson, 1998, pp. 89–92.

7. Quoted in "Vint Cerf," *Forbes*, October 6, 1997, p. S132 ff.

8. Quoted in Katie Hafner and Matthew Lyon, *Where Wizards Stay Up Late: The Origins of the Internet.* New York: Simon & Schuster, 1996, p. 139.

9. Quoted in Hafner and Lyon, *Where Wizards Stay Up Late,* p. 139.

10. Quoted in Hafner and Lyon, *Where Wizards Stay Up Late,* p. 137.

11. Quoted in Schick, *Current Biography Yearbook 1998,* pp. 89–92.

12. Quoted in Hafner and Lyon, *Where Wizards Stay Up Late,* p. 143.

13. Vint Cerf, "Commentary: Progressive Initiatives Seen for ACM." *Communications of the ACM,* October 1992, pp. S1 ff.

14. Quoted in Hafner and Lyon, *Where Wizards Stay Up Late,* p. 179.

15. Quoted in Hafner and Lyon, *Where Wizards Stay Up Late,* p. 138.

16. Quoted in Schick, *Current Biography Yearbook 1998,* pp. 89–92.

17. "Vint Cerf," *Forbes,* p. S132 ff.

18. Quoted in Herb Brody, "Net Cerfing," *Technology Review*, May–June 1998, p. 73 ff.

19. Quoted in Brody, "Net Cerfing," p. 73 ff.

20. Quoted in Charlotte Dunlap, "Vint Cerf," *Computer Reseller News*, November 15, 1998, p. 25 ff.

21. Quoted in Debbie L. Sklar, "The Bell Tolls for Vint Cerf," *America's Network*, August 15, 1998, p. 49.

Chapter 3: Tim Berners-Lee: Weaving the World Wide Web

22. Tim Berners-Lee, *Weaving the Web*. San Francisco: HarperSanFrancisco, 1999, p. 4.

23. Quoted in Joshua Quittner, "Network Designer Tim Berners-Lee," *Time*, March 29, 1999, p. 192 ff.

24. Berners-Lee, *Weaving the Web*, p. 10.

25. Berners-Lee, *Weaving the Web*, p. 20.

26. Berners-Lee, *Weaving the Web*, pp. 83–84.

27. Berners-Lee, *Weaving the Web*, p. 86.

28. Quoted in Ethirajan Anbarasan, "Tim Berners-Lee: The Web's Brainchild," *UNESCO Courier*, September 2000, p. 46 ff.

29. Berners-Lee, *Weaving the Web*, p. 123.

Chapter 4: Marc Andreessen: Netscape Changes the Landscape

30. Quoted in Rick Tetzeli, "What It's Really Like to Be Marc Andreessen." *Fortune*, December 9, 1996, p. 136 ff.

31. Tetzeli, "What It's Really Like to Be Marc Andreessen," p. 136 ff.

32. Quoted in Sara Hazlewood, "Andreessen: AOL's New Evangelist," *Business Journal*, April 2, 1999, p. 14.

33. Quoted in Rick Tetzeli and David Kirkpatrick, "The Concept of Being Always on Is a Very Powerful One," *Fortune*, October 9, 2000, p. 252.

34. Quoted in Gregory R. Gromov, "The Roads and Crossroads of Internet History." Available on-line at www.netvalley.com/intval web.html.

35. Quoted in Elizabeth A. Schick, ed., *Current Biography Yearbook 1997*, New York: H. W. Wilson, 1998, p. 12.

36. Alison Sprout, "The Rise of Netscape," *Fortune*, July 10, 1995, p. 140 ff.

37. Tetzeli, "What it's really like to be Marc Andreessen," p. 136 ff.

38. Quoted in Schick, *Current Biography Yearbook 1997*, p. 12.
39. Quoted in Gary Andrew Poole, "A Startup's Startup," *Forbes*, April 3, 2000, p. 111 ff.
40. Quoted in Poole, "A Startup's Startup," p. 111 ff.
41. Quoted in Carol Sliwa, "Andreessen Targets Web Outsource Model," *Computerworld*, September 25, 2000, p. 32.

Chapter 5: Jerry Yang: Gateway to the Web

42. Quoted in William Plummer, "The World at Their Fingertips," *People Weekly*, December 4, 1995, p. 123.
43. Quoted in Brent Schlender, "How a Virtuoso Plays the Web," *Fortune*, March 6, 2000, p. F-79 ff.
44. Quoted in Schlender, "How a Virtuoso Plays the Web," p. F-79 ff.
45. Quoted in Robert H. Reid, *Architects of the Web: 1,000 Days That Built the Future of Business*. New York: John Wiley, 1997 p. 246.
46. Quoted in Plummer, "The World at Their Fingertips," p. 123.
47. Jerry Yang, "Turn On, Type In and Drop Out," *Forbes*, December 1, 1997, p. S51 ff.
48. Quoted in Brent Schlender, "The Customer Is the Decision-Maker," *Fortune*, March 6, 2000, p. F-84 ff.
49. Quoted in Reid, *Architects of the Web*, p. 254.
50. Quoted in Amy Virshup, "Yahoo! How Two Stanford Students Created the Little Search Engine That Could," *Rolling Stone*, November 30, 1995, p. 16.
51. Quoted in *Marketing*, "Chief Yahoo," October 30, 1997, p. 23.
52. Quoted in Schick, *Current Biography Yearbook 1997*, p. 643.
53. Quoted in Schick, *Current Biography Yearbook 1997*, p. 643.
54. Reid, *Architects of the Web*, p. 265.
55. Quoted in Jeff Goodell, "Jerry Yang," *Rolling Stone*, March 30, 2000, p. 7 ff.
56. Quoted in Goodell, "Jerry Yang," p. 7 ff.
57. Quoted in Schlender, "How a Virtuoso Plays the Web," p. F-79 ff.
58. Yang, "Turn On, Type In and Drop Out," p. S51 ff.

Chapter 6: Jeff Bezos: The World's Biggest Bookstore

59. Quoted in Robert Spector, *Amazon.com: Get Big Fast.* New York: HarperCollins, 2000, p. 5.

60. Quoted in Spector, *Amazon.com*, p. 5.

61. Quoted in Spector, *Amazon.com*, pp. 6–7.

62. Quoted in Chip Bayers, "The Inner Bezos," *Wired*, March 1999. Available on-line at http://www.wired.com/wired/archives/7.03/bezos.html.

63. Quoted in Bayers, "The Inner Bezos."

64. Quoted in Spector, *Amazon.com*, p. 10.

65. Quoted in Spector, *Amazon.com*, p. 14.

66. Quoted in Spector, *Amazon.com*, p. 14.

67. Quoted in Alex Grove, "Surfing the Amazon," *Red Herring*, July 1, 1997. Available on-line at www.redherring.com.

68. Quoted in Spector, *Amazon.com*, pp. 30–31.

69. Quoted in Karen Southwick, "Interview with Jeff Bezos of Amazon.com," Upside.com, October 1, 1996. Available on-line at www.upside.com/texis/mvm/story?id=34712c154b.

70. Quoted in Spector, *Amazon.com*, p. 43.

71. Quoted in Spector, *Amazon.com*, p. 49.

72. Quoted in Spector, *Amazon.com*, p. 72.

73. Quoted in Spector, *Amazon.com*, p. 73.

74. Quoted in Spector, *Amazon.com*, p. 89.

75. Quoted in Spector, *Amazon.com*, p. 93.

76. Quoted in Spector, *Amazon.com*, pp. 92–93.

77. Quoted in, "Back to Being Amazon.Bomb," *Fortune*, June 26, 2000, p. 142.

78. Quoted in Adam Geller, "Old Story for New Economy Titans," *CanadianPress*, March 13, 2001.

Chapter 7: Pierre Omidyar: Commerce Through Community

79. Quoted in Gregory K. Ericksen, *Net Entrepreneurs Only: 10 Entrepreneurs Tell the Stories of Their Success.* New York: John Wiley, 2000, p. 172.

80. Quoted in Ericksen, *Net Entrepreneurs Only*, p. 164.

81. Quoted in Ericksen, *Net Entrepreneurs Only*, pp. 163–164.

82. Quoted in Ericksen, *Net Entrepreneurs Only*, p. 166.

83. Quoted in Randall E. Stross, *eBoys: The First Inside Account of Venture Capitalists at Work*. New York: Crown, 2000, p. 52.

84. Quoted in Adam Sachs, "The Billionaire Nobody Knows," *GQ*, May 2000, p. 235.

85. Quoted in Ericksen, *Net Entrepreneurs Only*, p. 175.

86. Quoted in Stross, *eBoys*, p. 177.

87. Quoted in Stross, *eBoys*, pp. 178–79.

88. Quoted in Stross, *eBoys*, p. 179.

89. Quoted in Adam Cohen, "Coffee with Pierre: Creating a Web Community Made Him Singularly Rich," *Time*, December 27, 1999, p. 78ff.

90. Quoted in Ericksen, *Net Entrepreneurs Only*, p. 168.

91. Quoted in Ericksen, *Net Entrepreneurs Only*, p. 165.

92. Sachs, "The Billionaire Nobody Knows," p. 233.

93. Quoted in Sachs, "The Billionaire Nobody Knows," p. 234.

Glossary

ARPA (Advanced Research Projects Agency), later **DARPA (Defense Advanced Research Projects Agency):** Government agencies that funded the development of the network first known as ARPAnet and later the Internet.

browser (or **Web browser**): A software program used to view pages on the World Wide Web and to navigate using hypertext links.

domain: An abbreviation used to specify the type of website (as in .com for commercial sites) or the site's location (as in uk for the United Kingdom).

dot-com: A company whose business depends on selling goods or services through the Internet. The term comes from the .com in the Web address.

e-commerce or **electronic commerce:** The buying and selling of goods or services using websites located on the Internet.

e-mail or **electronic mail:** The sending of messages between Internet users.

entrepreneur: A person who starts and runs his or her own business.

header: The part of a data packet (or an e-mail or news message) that describes who sent it and its intended recipient.

home page: The main page of a website that serves as an introduction and table of contents.

host computer: A computer system that runs websites or other services provided over the Internet.

HTML (Hypertext Markup Language): Special commands added to text files to format them for Web browsers, including headings, boldface, hypertext links, and graphics.

HTTP (Hypertext Transport Protocol): A set of specifications for how browsers and other programs retrieve information from the World Wide Web.

Initial Public Offering (IPO): The first offering of a company's stock to the public.

Internet: The worldwide connection of computer networks that use a common routing system called TCP/IP.

Internet Service Provider (ISP): A business that offers a connection to the Internet, usually for a monthly service charge.

Java: A computer programming language often used to add features to Web pages.

log on (or **log in**): To connect to a computer system, usually by giving a user ID and password.

mainframe: A large computer system such as those developed during the 1950s. Mainframes are still used today for large databases and business applications.

network: A connection of two or more computers linked so they can access each other's data or programs.

packet: The basic unit into which data is broken up before transmitting it on the Internet.

packet switching: The system by which packets are routed to their destination and reassembled into complete messages or documents.

portal: A website designed to provide convenient access to a variety of information links.

protocol: A set of specifications that describe how computers in a network will communicate.

router: A device that uses software to access a list of network routes and select the best path for outgoing data packets.

server: A computer that provides a resource to be shared by many users, such as a website or file storage space.

TCP/IP (Transmission Control Protocol/Internet Protocol): The basic method for moving data packets around the Internet.

URL (Uniform Resource Locator): The address used to locate a Web page, file, image, or other resource on the Internet.

venture capitalist: A person or firm who invests in new companies in exchange for a share in their ownership and future profits.

World Wide Web (the Web): A system that connects millions of interlinked pages containing hypertext, graphics, and other features over the Internet.

For Further Reading

Books

Tim Berners-Lee, *Weaving the Web*. San Francisco: HarperSanFrancisco, 1999. The inventor of the World Wide Web describes what led him to develop it and how he envisions its future.

Gregory K. Ericksen, *Net Entrepreneurs Only: 10 Entrepreneurs Tell the Stories of Their Success*. New York: John Wiley, 2000. Offers vivid accounts of risk takers who started Web-based businesses (and met with varying success). Includes a chapter on Pierre Omidyar, founder of eBay.

Harry Henderson, *Communications and Broadcasting*. New York: Facts On File, 1997. From the telegraph to the Internet, this collection of biographies of inventors explores the development and connection of ideas that changed the way people communicate.

———, *The Internet*. San Diego: Lucent Books, 1998. An overview of the many facets of the Internet including education, commerce, and new forms of community.

Robert H. Reid, *Architects of the Web: 1,000 Days That Built the Future of Business*. New York: John Wiley, 1997. Describes the inventors who have expanded the Web, adding capabilities such as live, streaming broadcasts, virtual reality, and new search engines. Includes chapters on Marc Andreessen and Jerry Yang.

Howard Rheingold, *The Virtual Community: Homesteading on the Electronic Frontier*. Reading, MA: Addison-Wesley, 1993. An important book about the social, rather than commercial, side of the Internet. Describes how people create lasting on-line communities.

Stephen Segaller, *Nerds 2.0.1: A Brief History of the Internet*. New York: TV Books, 1999. Based on a television special, this book gives clear and entertaining accounts of the people and events that led to the creation of today's world-spanning Internet.

Robert Spector, *Amazon.com: Get Big Fast*. New York: HarperCollins, 2000. A lively telling of the story of Jeff Bezos and the culture that grew up around Amazon.com. It also serves as a broader look at the "dot-com" world.

Websites

Amazon (www.amazon.com). Bills itself as the world's largest bookstore, founded by Jeff Bezos.

CyberAtlas (http://cyberatlas.internet.com). A site that provides extensive information and statistics about e-commerce.

eBay (www.ebay.com). The world's largest on-line auction site, founded by Pierre Omidyar.

Internet Society (www.isoc.org). Founded in 1992, the Internet Society is devoted to establishing technical standards, improving the Internet architecture, and educating the public about the Internet.

LoudCloud (www.loudcloud.com). The company founded by Marc Andreessen after Netscape was bought by America Online.

Worldwide Web Consortium (www.w3c.org). An international organization founded by Tim Berners-Lee and other developers of the World Wide Web. It plans future enhancements of the Web and deals with Web-related social issues.

Yahoo! (www.yahoo.com.) The world's largest Web directory, founded by Jerry Yang and David Filo.

WORKS CONSULTED

Books

Alan Freedman, *The Computer Desktop Encyclopedia*, 2nd ed. New York: AMACOM, 1999. A comprehensive dictionary of computer-related terms.

Katie Hafner and Matthew Lyon, *Where Wizards Stay Up Late: The Origins of the Internet.* New York: Simon & Schuster, 1996. Tells the story of scientists and engineers who used government backing to create ARPAnet, which eventually became the worldwide Internet. Includes accounts of the work of Vint Cerf and Robert Kahn in devising and implementing the Internet communications protocol.

Neil Randall, *The Soul of the Internet: Net Gods, Netizens and the Wiring of the World.* New York: International Thompson Computer Press, 1997. Details the development of the Internet and the programs that made it useful.

Donald Spencer, *The Timetable of Computers*, 2nd ed. Ormond Beach, FL: Camelot, 1999. An illustrated timeline of events in the history of computing.

Randall E. Stross, *eBoys: The First Inside Account of Venture Capitalists at Work.* New York: Crown, 2000. Describes the frenetic world of venture capitalists seeking to launch dot-coms at the height of the e-commerce boom.

Periodicals

Ethirajan Anbarasan, "Tim Berners-Lee: The Web's Brainchild," *UNESCO Courier,* September 2000.

Chip Bayers, "The Inner Bezos," *Wired,* March 1999. Available on-line at http://www.wired/archive/7.03/bezos.html.

Herb Brody, "Net Cerfing," *Technology Review,* May–June 1998.

Vint Cerf, "Commentary: Progressive Initiations Seen for ACM," *Communications of the ACM,* October 1992.

Adam Cohen, "Coffee with Pierre: Creating a Web Community Made Him Singularly Rich," *Time,* December 27, 1999.

Charlotte Dunlap, "Vint Cerf," *Computer Reseller News,* November 15, 1998.

Forbes, "Vint Cerf," October 6, 1997.

Fortune, "Back to Being Amazon.Bomb," June 26, 2000.

Adam Geller, "Old Story for New Economy Titans," *CanadianPress,* March 13, 2001.

Jeff Goodell, "Jerry Yang," *Rolling Stone*, March 30, 2000.

Alex Grove, "Surfing the Amazon," *Red Herring*, July 1, 1997. Available on-line at www.redherring.com.

Sara Hazlewood, "Andreessen: AOL's New Evangelist," *Business Journal*, April 2, 1999.

Marketing, "Chief Yahoo," October 30, 1997.

William Plummer, "The World at Their Fingertips," *People Weekly*, December 4, 1995.

Gary Andrew Poole, "A Startup's Startup," *Forbes*, April 3, 2000.

Joshua Quittner, "Network Designer Tim Berners-Lee," *Time*, March 29, 1999.

Adam Sachs, "The Billionaire Nobody Knows," *GQ*, May 2000.

Elizabeth A. Schick, ed., *Current Biography Yearbook 1997*. New York: H. W. Wilson, 1997.

Elizabeth A. Schick, ed., *Current Biography Yearbook 1998*. New York: H. W. Wilson, 1998.

Brent Schlender, "The Customer Is the Decision-Maker," *Fortune*, March 6, 2000.

Brent Schlender, "How a Virtuoso Plays the Web," *Fortune*, March 6, 2000.

Debbie L. Sklar, "The Bell Tolls for Vint Cerf," *America's Network*, August 15, 1998.

Carol Sliwa, "Andreessen Targets Web Outsource Model," *Computerworld*, September 25, 2000.

Alison Sprout, "The Rise of Netscape," *Fortune*, July 10, 1995.

Rick Tetzeli, "What It's Really Like to Be Marc Andreessen," *Fortune*, December 9, 1996.

Rick Tetzeli and David Kirkpatrick, "The Concept of Being Always on Is a Very Powerful One," *Fortune*, October 9, 2000.

Amy Virshup, "Yahoo! How Two Stanford Students Created the Little Search Engine That Could," *Rolling Stone*, November 30, 1995.

Jerry Yang, "Turn On, Type In and Drop Out," *Forbes*, December 1, 1997.

Internet Sources

Gregory R. Gromov, "The Roads and Crossroads of Internet History." www.netvalley.com/intvalweb.html.

Nathaniel Hawthorne, *The House of the Seven Gables*, http://eldred.ne. mediaone.net/nh/sg.html.

Leonard Kleinrock, "Information Flow in Large Communication Nets." [Ph.D. Thesis Proposal], www.lk.cs.ucla.edu/LK/Bib/REPORT/PhD.

Karen Southwick, "Interview with Jeff Bezos of Amazon.com," Upside.com, October 1, 1996. www.upside.com/texis/mvm/story?id= 34712c154b.

Websites

Computer Industry Almanac (www.c-i-a.com). Offers a variety of statistics on computer and Internet use.

Investorwords (www.investorwords.com). A site providing definitions for five thousand business, financial, and investment terms.

Upside.com (www.upside.com). An e-commerce and technology news site.

ZD Webopedia (www.zdwebopedia.com). An on-line hyperlinked encyclopedia of computing terms.

INDEX

Advanced Research Projects Agency
    (ARPA), 16–17, 25
Aiken, Howard, 15
Albright, Madeleine, 59
Alexander Graham Bell award, 32
Amazon.com, 10, 70
    beginnings of, 21, 76–77
    complexity of, 55
    cost effectiveness of, 75
    financing of, 77–79
    first public stock offering of, 80–81
    focus on customer service, 79–80
    Netscape and, 60
    odd books on, 78
American Booksellers Association
    (ABA), 76
America Online (AOL), 20, 53–54
    bought by Time-Warner, 67
    Yahoo! and, 62–63
Andreessen, Marc, 46–56
    childhood of, 46–47
    as entrepreneur, 9, 42
    Mosaic and, 20
Apple Computer, 61, 84
ARPAnet, 17, 25
ASAP (magazine)
    on Yahoo! success story, 67
Atari, 61
Atomic Energy Commission, 71
Auction Web, 85

Babbage, Charles, 14
Bankers Trust Company, 73
Bank of America, 51
Baran, Paul, 17
Barksdale, Jim, 51
Barnes & Noble, 74–75
BASIC (programming language), 56
Benchmark, 88
Bendix G-15 (computer), 24–25
Berners-Lee, Tim, 9, 20
    childhood of, 34–35
    data management flow and, 35–36,
        38
    as steward of Web, 42–45
    Time magazine and, 45

Bezos, Jeff, 21, 74, 76–78, 80–82
    awards and scholarship of, 72–73
    backing for on-line bookstore, 75
    belief in e-commerce, 79
    childhood of, 10, 70–72
    "Infinity Cube" and, 71
    technical and financial skills of, 73
Bezos, Mackenzie, 76
Bezos, Miguel, 70
Bina, Eric, 47–48
Bolt, Beranek and Newman (BBN),
    17
Borders, 74–75
Boulder, Colorado, 76

Cerf, Muriel, 24
Cerf, Vinton Thruston, 24
Cerf, Vinton "Vint," 9, 21–22, 26–27,
    33–34
    ARPAnet and, 28
    awards to, 32
    childhood of, 10, 24
    as "father of the Internet", 23
    hearing impairment and, 29–30
    interest in programming and,
        24–25
    as professor at Stanford University,
        28
    as Renaissance man, 32
    TCP/IP protocols and, 19
CERN
    need for data management, 36
    Tim Berners-Lee and, 20
Cisco Systems, 61
Clark, Jim, 48
Clinton, Bill, 32
Communications Decency Act, 31
Communications Revolution, 8,
    12–13
CompuServe, 20
computers
    cold war and, 16
    data storing capacity of, 36–37
    early designs and uses, 14
    first "worm" and, 19
    modem, 16

operating systems and, 17
transistor and, 16–17
vacuum tubes and, 15
"Confessions of a Hearing-Impaired
Engineer" (Vinton Cerf), 29
Corporation for Research Initiatives,
30
Crocker, Steve, 24–26
Crown Books, 74

DARPA (early Internet agency), 71
D. E. Shaw Company
backing for on-line bookstore,
75–76
e-commerce and, 74
investment in on-line bookstore, 71
Digital Equipment Corporation
(DEC), 19
Dillon, Eric, 78

ebay, 10, 21, 83
Amazon.com and, 80
Auction Web and, 86–87
financing and, 88
naming of, 88
public stock offering of, 89–91
and Yahoo!, 68
ebay Foundation, 93
Eckert, J. Presper, 9, 15
e-commerce
Amazon.com and, 70, 74–75
credit cards and, 77
dot-coms and, 21–22
eShop and, 84
Jeff Bezos and, 74
Webvan and, 21
Yahoo! and, 64
Edison, Thomas, 8, 12
Emanuel School (London), 34–35
ENIAC (computer), 15
Enquire, 38
Enquire Within upon Everything
(encyclopedia), 34
Equinet, 73
eShop, 84, 86–87
Estrin, Jerry, 25

Filo, David, 21, 58–60
Fitel, 73
Forbes (magazine)
on Yahoo! success story, 67

Gates, Bill, 52–53
General Magic, 85
Geocities, 65
Gise, Jacklyn, 70
Gise, Preston, 71
Goldman-Sachs, 89

Harvard University, 15
Hawthorne, Nathaniel
on electricity and society, 13
Hearst publications, 51
Hennessy, John, 68
Hirsch, Harvey, 73
Hollerith, Herman, 14
House of the Seven Gables, The
(Hawthorne), 13
HTML (Hypertext Markup
Language), 20
HTTP (Hypertext Transfer Protocol),
40
"Hypertext 91," 42

Industrial Revolution, 8
information
difference between data and,
38–39
storage, retrieval, and management
of, 14
"Information Flow in Large
Communications Nets"
(Kleinrock), 17
Information Revolution, 12, 13–22
physical commerce and, 70
changes in social and economic
landscape and, 9
Ink Development, 84
Interface Message Processor (IMP),
17–18
International Business Machines
(IBM), 14, 19, 25
International Conference on
Computer Communications, 28
International Network Working
Group, 28
Internet
beginning of, 8–11
browsers and, 20
commerce and, 21, 70
early connections to, 19
first message over, 18
"Galactic Network," 17

government regulation and, 30–31
hypertext and, 39–40
"Interplanetary Internet" and, 31
remote procedure call (RPC) and, 40
routers and, 19
search engines, 57–58
social concerns, 30, 43–45
"Web portals" and, 21
Internet Explorer, 20, 52
Internet Protocol (IP), 19
Internet Service Providers (ISP), 20
Internet Society, 30
inventions
    Thomas Edison and, 8
    radio, 12
    social and economic implications
      of, 9

Java (programming language), 52
Jet Propulsion Lab (JPL), 31
Johns Hopkins University Medical
    Center, 83
Jurassic Park (movie), 48

Kahn, Robert
    awards and, 32
    TCP/IP protocols and, 19, 28
Kaphan, Sheldon, 76, 77
Kleinrock, Leonard, 17, 18
    first computer network and, 26–28
Kline, Charlie, 18
Kmart, 65
Knight-Ridder, 51
Koogle, Tim
    mergers and, 67–68
    resignation from Yahoo!, 68
    as Yahoo! CEO, 63

Lake Tahoe, Nevada, 76
Lands' End, 56
Licklider, J. C. R., 17
Linux (operating system), 52
Los Altos, California, 66
LoudCloud, 54–56
Lycos (search engine), 57

MacDraw (program), 84
Macintosh (computer), 20
Manchester University (Britain), 34,
    35

Mark I (computer), 15, 34
Marshall Spaceflight Center
    (Alabama), 72
Mauchly, John, 9, 15
McCracken, Ed, 49
MCI, 30
Merrill Lynch, 74
Microsoft Corporation, 52–53
    monopoly and, 53
    Yahoo! and, 67
Minor, Halsey, 74
MIT, 26
Montgomery Ward, 70
Moritz, Mike, 61
Morse, Samuel, 8, 12
Mosaic, 20, 48
Mosaic Communications
    Corporation, 49
Mountain View, California, 49

National Center for Supercomputing
    Applications (NCSA), 20, 47,
    49–50
National Medal of Technology, 32
Netscape Communications, 54
    established, 49
    public stock offering of, 51
    relationship with Yahoo!, 60, 64
Netscape Navigator (Mosaic
    NetScape)
    awards for, 50
    competition and, 52–53
    corporate Web design and, 51–52
    "Mozilla," 9
    universal net accessibility and, 20
Network Measurement Center, 26
networks, 25
    addresses and, 40
    common language and, 16, 36–37
    hypertext and, 20, 39–40
    links and, 37–38
    methods of routing, 17
    military defense and, 16
    protocols and routers and, 19,
      26–28
    TCP/IP and, 28–29

Omidyar, Pam, 85
Omidyar, Pierre, 86–90, 93
    childhood of, 10, 83–84

on community building, 91–92
computer graphics and special
effects and, 85
development of computer pen and,
84
Pez candy dispensers and, 85
Oracle, 61

Palmetto High School, 72
Plain Old Telephone System (POTS),
31
Portland, Oregon, 76
Princeton University, 73

Queen's College at Oxford University
(Britain), 36

RAND Corporation, 17
Reid, Robert
on Yahoo! partnership, 66–67
Roberts, Larry, 17, 26

San Francisco, California, 48
Sears, 70
Seattle, Washington, 86
Sequoia Capital, 61
Silicon Graphics, 48
Silicon Valley, 48
Skoll, Jeff, 87
Soviet Union, 16
Sprout, Alison
on Clark-Andreessen partnership,
48
Stanford Research Institute (SRI), 18
Stanford University, 68
Jeff Skoll and, 87
Jerry Yang and, 58–61
Vint Cerf and, 25
Stross, Randall
on eBay stock-offering party, 90
Supreme Court, 31

TCP/IP, 19, 28
telecommunications, 12
telegraph, 8
news and financial markets and, 13
similarities to computer, 12
telephone
democratization of
communications and, 13

method of passing messages on, 12
modem and, 16
Thorstenberg, Sigrid, 25
Torvalds, Linus, 52
Transmission Control Protocol (TCP),
19
Tufts University, 84

Uniform Resource Locator (URL),
40
United States, 16
UNIVAC (computer), 9, 15
Universal Resource Identifier (URI),
40
University of California at Los Angeles
(UCLA), 18, 25
University of California at Santa
Barbara (UCSB), 18
University of Illinois, 47, 49
University of Utah, 18
Unix (operating system), 52
U.S. Department of Defense, 25
Sputnik and, 16
USENET (Netnews), 19

Walt Disney Company, 66
Washington, D.C., 28
Werner, Ursula, 72
Whitman, Meg, 68, 88
Windows (operating system), 20
Wired (magazine)
on Yahoo! success story, 67
Woolworth, F. W., 70
World War II
enemy codes and, 14–15
World Wide Web, 34
beginning of, 9
browsers, 9, 20, 41, 58
components of, 41
first visualization of, 35
hypertext and, 20, 39–40
immediate investment news on,
73–74
launching of, 40–50
regulation of, 43–44
as a social system, 83
Web pages and, 45
"Web portals" and, 21
World Wide Web Consortium (W3C),
42–45

Yahoo!, 10, 61–68
  ebay and, 68
  e-commerce relationships and, 64
  "Jerry's Guide to the World Wide
    Web," 60–61
  Microsoft and, 67
  My Yahoo! and, 64
  naming of, 62
  as oldest "Web portal," 21, 58
  public stock offering of, 64–65
  success story of, 66–67

  venture capital for, 61–63
Yang, Akiko, 66
Yang, Chi-Yuan. *See* Yang, Jerry
Yang, Jerry, 21, 57, 59–60, 62–65, 67
  childhood of, 10, 58
  on life as a successful entrepreneur,
    68
  quitting college, 61
  wealth and, 66
Yang, Ken, 58
Yang, Lily, 58

PICTURE CREDITS

ABOUT THE AUTHOR

Harry Henderson is a freelance writer specializing in computer-related and scientific subjects including historical, biographical, and reference works. He has written a variety of books about computer languages, computer communications, and the Internet. These include *The Internet* (Lucent, 1998), *Issues in the Information Age* (Lucent, 1999), *Communications and Broadcasting* (Facts On File, 1997), and *Career Opportunities in Computers and Cyberspace* (Facts On File, 1999). He lives in El Cerrito, California, with his wife, Lisa Yount, also a prolific nonfiction author.